BUSINESS IS A BATTLEFIELD: TALES FROM THE TRENCHES

KAREN P. JOHNSON

Copyright © 2015 Karen P. Johnson

Published by K Johnson Consulting, LLC
No part of this publication may be reproduced, stored in a retrieval system, or transmitted in any form or by any means, electronic, mechanical, photocopying, recording, scanning, or otherwise, except as permitted under Section 107 or 108 of the 1976 United States Copyright Act, without either the prior written permission of the publisher. Requests to the author for permission should be addressed to Karen Johnson, P O Box 791, Benton, LA 71006.

Limit of Liability/Disclaimer of Warranty - While the publisher and author have used their best efforts in preparing this book, they make no representations or warranties with respect to the accuracy or completeness of the contents of this book and specifically disclaim any implied warranties of merchantability or fitness for a particular purpose. No warranty may be created or extend by sales representatives or written sales materials. The advice and Strategies contained herein may not be suitable for your situation. You should consult with a professional where appropriate. Neither the publisher nor author shall be liable for any loss of profit or any other commercial damages, including but not limited to special, incidental, consequential or other damages.

Readers should be aware that Internet Web sites offered as citations and/or sources for further information may have changed or disappeared between the time this was written and when it is read.

ISBN-13: 978-0-9972054-1-1

Table of Contents

Introduction i

Know Yourself! 1

Do What You Do Well! 15

Be Generous With Value! 23

Success (or Lack Thereof) is a Result of Your Choices!...37

Choose Who You Listen To Carefully! 72

Ask For What You Want! 81

Choose Your Partners Carefully! 94

Work Hard! 108

Choose Your Team Members Carefully! 119

In Closing 145

Forward

I'd like to thank all of the businessmen and businesswomen who consented to be interviewed for this book. I won't list the names because some requested that their names not be used, and I do not want to omit anyone. Thank you all for your patience and your generosity with your time.

A special Thank You goes to Brian Tracy for taking his valuable time to preview this book.

"This fast-moving, enjoyable book describes exactly what you have to do to be successful in any business."
Brian Tracy – Author, *How The Best Leaders Lead*

INTRODUCTION

"Charm is deceptive, and beauty is fleeting; but a woman who fears the Lord is to be praised. Honor her for all that her hands have done, and let her works bring her praise at the city gate."
- Proverbs 31:30-31

I've always wanted to write a book. I've been an avid reader as long as I can remember, and it just seemed like a natural progression to write one. I mean, really, how hard can it be? Ummm.... It was hard! The first draft was three years in the making, and it is really not a very long book. What took me so long? For starters, I looked back over my career and decided that if I wrote only from my own experiences, I would bore you to tears. It finally occurred to me that while I personally might not have a lot of great stories in me, there are lots of people who do. I reached out to the business community and asked them for their stories. Almost everyone I asked agreed to help. The people in Louisiana are generous with everything, including their time.

These tales came from the day-to-day experiences of real businesspeople mostly in Louisiana. I took some literary license with some actual situations, some for the flow of the story, and some out of respect for the anonymity of those who asked that their names or company names not be used. If you recognize yourself or someone else in a negative light, rest assured it is an unintended coincidence. Some of the vignettes are composites of more than one situation combined to make the point.

Thank you for reading, and I'll see you on the battlefield.

CHAPTER ONE
KNOW YOURSELF!

"Knowing yourself is the beginning of all wisdom."
- Aristotle

"If you know the enemy and know yourself you need not fear the results of a hundred battles."
- Sun Tzu

"This is one thing I won't miss when I retire!" Augusta ("Gus" to her friends and colleagues) mumbled to herself as she inched along Interstate 12. The morning found Gus at a creeping pace approaching the Amite River Bridge, which connects Livingston Parish to East Baton Rouge Parish and the City of Baton Rouge. Traffic flow in Baton Rouge had never been anything to write home about, and on August 29, 2005, Hurricane Katrina irrevocably made her vicious mark on the area by pursuing tens of thousands of New Orleans residents north. Many never went back, and Gus was convinced that each and every one was sitting right there with her at mile marker 14. Of course, retiring wasn't even in the plans. Gus had found her calling when she stumbled upon business coaching, and as long as her short legs and quick wits could keep up, she would keep coaching!

Gus settled back into the comfortable leather seats of her Lexus ES350, a gift to herself after her eight-year-old Avalon became too tired and tattered to carry on, and began reminiscing about the roads she had travelled, bridges she had crossed and businesses she had helped in her ten years serving as a Business Coach. She glanced to the left and saw a familiar profile in the driver's seat of the car beside her. She smiled as she thought about how far Sherry Nivens had come since their first meeting 3 years ago.

Sherry's Story

To the outside world Sherry always appeared confident and professional but in reality, just three short years ago, she was terrified! Recently divorced, with a seven-year-old daughter, Sherry had found herself increasingly dissatisfied with her job. Having spent three years with Ernst & Young, a "Big 6" accounting firm, and a total of seven years with two different local firms, Sherry believed passionately that public accounting was her "calling" and that it was time to strike out on her own. But where, oh where, to start? Sherry put on a cheerful face, and said goodbye to her daughter, Marie, as she bounded out of the car and raced down the sidewalk to "Mimi" waiting at the door to greet her. Marie always looked forward to staying overnight with Mimi while Sherry went to her monthly Pokeno night. This group had been together for more than five years, and each of the ladies brought a unique perspective to the gatherings. Sherry knew she could count on receiving a great deal of moral support, but it would take more than moral support to get her where she needed to be.

Halfway through the evening, Wendy leaned over and said "Earth to Sherry, Earth to Sherry, come in Sherry. Where ARE you girl? I've covered the last three cards for you but you are still well on your way to winning the booby prize (the consolation prize for the player who won the fewest chips during the evening)."

Sherry chuckled and said, "I'm sorry Wendy...I'm just trying to figure out how to get started building my own accounting firm. I know that I do an excellent job on tax preparation and audits, but I just don't have any idea how to get clients. Why don't they teach that at LSU? I did well in my marketing classes, but to tell you the truth they never addressed the issues that face sole practitioners. I could probably prepare a marketing campaign for a company like GE, but I don't know what to do for myself."

"You need to talk to Gus Parker" Wendy responded. "She is my husband's coach. He has been working with her for a little over a year. In the last six months he has had so much growth in his business that he had to hire two more associates and a legal secretary."

"Hasn't he practiced by himself for the last few years?"

"Yes, but it wasn't by choice. He just couldn't get enough clients to grow his business like he wanted to."

"So, what did he do differently last year?"

"I told you! He hired a coach! Now pay attention and play your own card!"

The conversation whirled around in her head the rest of the night. Sherry did, in fact, win the booby prize, since her concentration did not improve dramatically and Wendy's assistance dropped off sharply. The booby prize was a Brian Tracy book entitled *Focal Point: A Proven System to Simplify Your Life, Double Your Productivity, and Achieve All Your Goals*. "How appropriate," Sherry mused. " I come in dead last because I'm trying to figure out how I'm going to reach my goals, and the prize is a book written to help me reach my goals. And didn't Wendy say that Gus is a Business Coach? Maybe this is something I need to do." As she readied for bed that night Sherry wondered if she could afford to have a coach. As she drifted off to sleep she wondered if she could afford not to.

A New Beginning

Monday morning brought rain to the capital city. Nothing new there! What WAS new was Sherry's determination to strike out on her own. After several attempts and false starts, she finally finished her resignation letter and carefully placed it on the desk of Harland Masters, one of the partners of the firm. She would have preferred delivering it to him personally, but he was out of town at a conference and wouldn't be back for another week. She knew his secretary would open the envelope and relay the message. Anyway, Harland knew she had been trying to make this leap for a few months. There were just too many "differences in management philosophy" with the other partner for Sherry to seriously contemplate pursuing a partnership here. Her best choice was to go out on her own and do things her way. The problem was that she didn't know what her way was.

With determination born of desperation, Sherry reached in her briefcase for the slightly battered business card Wendy had given her at the Pokeno night. She stared at the card for several minutes, as if by force of will she could draw the inspiration she needed from the words written there. Finally, with slightly trembling hands, she dialed the number.

"GP Business Coaching of Baton Rouge where we Focus on the Points that Matter! In what direction can I point you?"

The enthusiasm of the ageless voice on the other end of the line took Sherry by surprise. " Uh, I, Uh, think I need a Business Coach," she stammered.

"Well, you've called the right place," the chipper voice responded. "May I ask you a few questions to get you started?"

"Sure," said Sherry.

After getting her name and address, Marilly, the owner of the chipper voice, asked Sherry, "Will you tell me how long you have been in your current business, and what your position is?" "Well," confessed Sherry, "I haven't exactly started yet. I just turned my resignation in to my current employer. I gave two weeks' notice, but I'm pretty sure they will show me the door when they read the letter."

"Oh isn't that exciting!" Marilly squealed. "Not being shown the door, of course, but starting your own business!"

"I guess it should be," Sherry responded. "But to tell the truth, I mostly feel scared and alone."

"You aren't alone anymore, dear, you are with GP Business Coaching. And you are in luck. We have a brand new Roundtable group starting Wednesday, the day after tomorrow. There is just one spot available and if you want you can join the group, assuming of course there aren't any potential competitors already in there."

Marilly walked Sherry through the rest of the enrollment process, chatting the whole time about how much she was going to enjoy the coaching process. She was so enthusiastic that Sherry couldn't help but wonder if she was for real. She carried on about the Roundtable members being her accountability group, her mastermind group, and how she would get a DISC assessment, have action plans, and takeaways, and so forth, that Sherry was almost relieved when the conversation came to an end. Most of the time she didn't know what Marilly was talking about. She didn't want to show her ignorance by asking, so she just murmured "yes" and "how wonderful" whenever it seemed appropriate. When she put the receiver back on the phone cradle, she looked up to see the "other partner" standing in her doorway. From the look on the woman's face, Sherry knew her earlier prediction was coming to fruition.

Getting Started and Going Public

At 11:30 the next morning, Sherry pulled into the parking lot at On the Border Mexican Restaurant on Corporate Boulevard. This restaurant was one of Wendy's favorite lunch spots. Wendy had to be mindful of taking long lunches, and this restaurant was great about getting patrons in and out quickly. Sherry had already been seated when Wendy bounded onto the glassed in patio area, bubbling over with excitement. Sherry had called her last night and told her the big news about her newly found freedom and the Roundtable group she had joined.

Sherry couldn't help but smile when she saw Wendy. Wendy was only 5'3", but her personality took up the entire room. Her smile was so big it was almost a force of nature, and apparently her hairdresser had not gotten the word that big hair was "out". She sported a cashmere sweater in the brightest shade of fuchsia Sherry had ever seen, paired with a pencil thin skirt with swirls of fuchsia, chartreuse and ocean blue. Around her neck was draped a coordinating scarf and she wore earrings and necklaces that would have made a Romanian gypsy proud. Sherry wouldn't even try to imagine wearing that combination, but she had to admit, it worked on Wendy.

Wendy enveloped Sherry in a hug, bumping the man at the next table with her luggage-sized purse in the process. She laughed her apologies to the gentleman whose scowl could not remain when tackled by the force of Wendy's grin. She settled into her chair and immediately began bombarding Sherry with questions. "Where is your office going to be? What does Marie think about it? Do you have any clients yet?"

"Hold on…hold on…One question at a time!"

Sherry laughed. "First... I've found a nice executive suite just down the street. The rent includes a shared reception area and access to a conference room on a first reserved - first served basis. There is a full-time receptionist who is also available for clerical assistance. They also have reliable high speed Internet and plenty of offices available in case I need to expand."

"Ooooooh!" Wendy exclaimed. "You've just started and you are already expanding! Maybe you don't need that coach after all!"

"Not so fast. I said in case I need to expand. I really don't expect to need more space, but it's there if I do. Besides, if this coach is as good as you say she is, then maybe I'll need more room sooner rather than later."

As the waitress brought the "fajitas for two" the ladies always ordered, Wendy turned the conversation to her latest exploits as marketing and public relations director for the area's largest privately owned manufacturing firm. Sherry was glad to think about something else for a while.

Sherry Learns About Herself

Wednesday came around faster than Sherry thought possible. Tuesday night she had been so engrossed in the booby prize book that before she realized how long she had been reading, she heard the cuckoo clock in the living room announce that midnight had arrived. Reluctantly, she closed the cover on the book. It simply would not do to show up to her first Roundtable session with dark circles under her eyes. Reading the book had done her some good though. Instead of fretting about where she would find clients, she concentrated on the practical down to earth ideas Brian Tracy revealed in his FocalPoint book. Maybe Wendy was right. Maybe she didn't need a coach, and everything she needed to know she could just get right from this book. But she had committed to the group, and more importantly, she had already paid the fee, so she would at least go to the first meeting and see what it was all about. Besides, she had completed the DISC ® assessment that was required for the first meeting and she was looking forward to learning what it all meant.

The elevator ride to the seventh floor of the North Bank Tower found Sherry alternating between excitement and fear. What if she was the only person starting a business from scratch? What if everybody else already knew what an accountability group was? What if she couldn't find the bathrooms? "Good grief Sherry!" she thought. "Get a hold of yourself, this isn't kindergarten!" She stood up straight, wiped non-existing lint off her jacket, pushed her shoulders back and exited the elevator the picture of confidence and professionalism. No one would ever guess she was trembling in her Pradas.

Sherry was a bit surprised to see that she was the last one to arrive. Marilly had told her there were seven other participants in the group, and Sherry quickly counted eight people in the room. That meant the coach was already there too. DARN! In the back of her mind she could hear her father saying, "If you are not ten minutes early, you are late!" Without realizing it, Sherry had just snagged her first "take away" from coaching. From this point forward she would always be early for meetings. In the ensuing years she would gain a reputation for being punctual, precise and professional. That reputation had its genesis on the threshold of Gus Parker's conference room.

Sherry recognized the woman in the gray pin striped suit as Gus Parker, the Business Coach of whom Wendy had spoken so highly. Even if she hadn't recognized her from her picture on the business card, as well as the website, the fact that she was wearing a GP Business Coaching nametag was a good first clue. The other people in the room were wearing lanyards with nametags around their necks. There was one lanyard left on the table, next to the bottled waters. Sherry tried to unobtrusively pick it up and slip into the room unnoticed, but that was not to be. Gus spied her from across the room and politely extricated herself from the cluster of people engaged in an animated conversation and briskly walked over with a welcoming smile. Sherry was struck by how, she struggled for the right word...., normal that's it …normal, Gus looked. Shouldn't the "super-coach" Wendy have described look, well, super?

The hour and a half interactive session flew by, and Sherry was amazed and excited about what she had learned. The Title of the session was "Know Yourself," and the content consisted of a thorough review of a behavioral assessment each participant had completed. The assessment report was generated from Sherry's answers to a battery of questions. Several members of the group laughed about how random the questions seemed, how some just didn't have a clear answer and that they just couldn't see how those questions could result in such a detailed and accurate assessment. Sherry had to admit that for the most part, the assessment was dead on. In fact one of the participants, she thought his name was John, proclaimed that it was "eerily accurate". Gus encouraged anyone who felt like the assessment was not on target to have someone who knew them very well to review it and give an opinion. "The assessment isn't perfect, of course." Gus opined, "But so far, I've never had anyone come back and tell me that the person who knows them best thought it was wrong. Usually my clients have been a bit chagrined to tell me that the other person read the report and laughed because it was so much on target."

The most astonishing part of the whole session was not learning about her personal communication preferences, though that was very interesting. The real "aha" moments centered on recognizing some communication styles of other people in her life, both personal and professional. Could it be that the ongoing conflict she had with Amanda, the "other partner" as she usually referred to her, stemmed from a clash of communication styles? Sherry was almost sorry that she wouldn't have the opportunity to apply some of her newfound knowledge to her relationship with Amanda. Almost!

Know Yourself! Action Steps

1. If you've never taken a DISC Assessment find a Business Coach or a Human Resources Professional who can deliver the assessment and meet with you for a detailed debrief.

2. Share your preferred communication style with those people you interact with professionally and personally.

Consider whether your business would benefit by having key employees become more adept at identifying the preferred communication styles for themselves and their team.

CHAPTER TWO
DO WHAT YOU DO WELL!

"You can only become truly accomplished at something you love. Don't make money your goal. Instead pursue the things you love doing and then do them so well that people can't take their eyes off of you."
- Maya Angelou

"Perfection is not attainable, but if we chase perfection we can catch excellence."
-Vince Lombardi

A honk from the car behind startled Gus back into awareness of her surroundings. She was slightly confused at first, since traffic had not moved and she was not holding anyone up. She looked in her rearview mirror and saw the kind face and big smile of Dr. Prem Menon. "What was he doing in this mess? He doesn't live out this way." Of course, Dr. Menon was so active in educating and serving the public in his specialty that it really shouldn't have surprised her to see him.

Dr. Prem Menon, Baton Rouge Louisiana

Gus first met Dr. Menon when he was the speaker at a local civic club. He was sharing with the club the outcome of the Free Asthma and Allergy Camp in Cochin India. When Gus heard the story, she was so impressed with Dr. Menon that she invited him to lunch at her favorite restaurant, Mansurs on the Boulevard. Over the best gumbo in Baton Rouge and the restaurant's unbeatable Warm Duck Salad, Dr. Menon told Gus how he came to be one of the most well respected Allergists/Immunologists in the country.

Dr. Menon had come to the United States from his native India almost three decades previously. The Reserve Bank of India allowed him and his wife each $8.00. Who knows how the powers that be decided that $8.00 was the right amount, but since the Indian currency he had in his pocket was virtually worthless, Dr. Menon was glad to have the $8.00. Dr. Menon brought with him a tenacity and work ethic that rivals the attitudes of the pioneers. He also brought his personal philosophy of "Do One Thing and Do it Well".

Dr. Menon's introduction to medicine in the United States was a pediatric residency at Louisiana State University Medical Center in New Orleans, Louisiana, followed by a fellowship in Allergy and Immunology at the LSU Medical Center in Shreveport and a stint in Immunology Research at Tulane, back in New Orleans. During these early years of his career, Dr. Menon was fully focused on Allergy and Immunology Clinical and Bench Research (research on nonhuman subjects). He published twelve full-length papers and thirty-three abstracts in peer reviewed Allergy, Asthma and Immunology Journals.

The Entrepreneurship Bug

During this time Dr. Menon caught a bug. This bug was life-changing and there was no medicine to treat it. This was the bug of Entrepreneurism, and the only way to treat it was to tackle it head on. Half measures would not do, and part time would not suffice. But, alas, some bugs cannot be cured. Dr. Menon knew that conducting research, presenting at clinical forums, and training young doctors was important, but to try to do all of that would spread him too thin and dilute his efforts. Justice would not have been done to the research or to his patients.

During the Christmas season of 1990, Dr. Menon

established the Asthma, Allergy and Immunology Center on Flanders Drive in Baton Rouge, Louisiana. His friends, colleagues and employers past and present told him he was crazy to do it. He couldn't have private practice and hold a research position as well. Dr. Menon agreed and turned his back on the research. He let go of a guaranteed and relatively predictable career path in favor of the unpredictable, and often rocky, path of the entrepreneur. He was determined to "Do one thing and do it well!"

Gus didn't know the whole of Dr. Menon's story, but she knew enough to have a great deal of admiration for him. He certainly lived up to his motto. He also relished the challenge of doing what naysayers claimed couldn't be done. He didn't come fifteen thousand miles from Calicut, Kerala, India to turn away from his passion, just because it might be hard. And hard it was.

The field of Allergy, Asthma and Immunology is not exactly crowded. In fact, at the time he opened his office in Baton Rouge, he could count on one hand the number of doctors in town who shared his field. The others were bound to notice the new kid in town. To say he was not greeted with open arms would be putting it mildly. Instead of welcoming an accomplished colleague into the area, some of his fellow Allergist/Immunologists scorned him. One of them called his office and sneered, "What is this…a joke? I've been in this town for thirty years, and this guy knows nobody!

What does he think he is going to do?"

Dr. Menon and his dedicated staff, which at the time consisted of himself, his office manager, and one LPN, set out to show what he would do. Always repeating the Mantra "Do One thing and Do it Well", they set out to make sure that no one in Dr. Menon's proximity ever again died from Asthma.

Making the Most of the Time Available

During the first couple of months, Dr. Menon saw an average of two patients per day. That left plenty of time each day for other activities, and he didn't let that time go to waste. He capitalized on the opportunity to make rounds visiting area doctors and pharmacists. He even managed to wrangle invitations to speak at conventions of doctors, nurses and pharmacists. He was relentless in pursuing credentialing as a provider for several insurance companies. One in particular kept telling him "no" because they had all the providers they needed for the number of patients they served in the area. Finally he got a break! One of the doctors, who had been on the "provider list" for several years, opted not to renew his contract. The insurance company executive remembered Dr. Menon's repeated efforts to be included on this list and made the call that helped Dr. Menon's practice turn the corner. Dr. Menon never knew if the other doctor really meant to pull out or if she was just trying to negotiate for more favorable terms. Either way, it was the break he had been looking for, and the influx of patients put his practice in the black for the first time.

In the early years of his practice, Dr. Menon accepted Medicaid and Medicare patients out of necessity. Many doctors in his field of expertise refuse to accept those patients for several reasons, not the least of which is the relatively low reimbursement rates. When times were lean, those patients sometimes made the difference between Dr. Menon going in the hole or coming out with money at the end of the month. Now that his practice is well established and he can pick and choose with whom he works, Dr. Menon still accepts those Medicaid and Medicare patients out of a sense of gratitude for the program which helped him when he needed help the most. Furthermore, turning away those patients would be contrary to his philosophy of doing one thing and doing it well. That philosophy wouldn't allow him to turn his back on those who needed help the most and were the least likely to be able to get it.

Over the years Dr. Menon continued to grow his practice. He often told those around him to follow their passions and not to worry about the money, it would come. Dr. Menon did exactly that. Since 1992, he has donated nebulizers to schools in East Baton Rouge and Tangipahoa parishes. He established a full time free Asthma and Allergy Clinic in Cochin, India in 1995 and conducted free Asthma and Allergy camps in India for six years. He has participated in, or sponsored, countless medical and humanitarian missions in the USA and abroad. In fact, the free Asthma clinic in India is still in operation seven days a week and has expanded its services to include other medical conditions. What does he think he is going to do, indeed!

Do What You Do Well!: Action Steps

1. Ask at least five coworkers what they see that you are particularly adept in. Determine whether you are making the most of those areas of expertise. If not, make a change.

2. Ask at least three friends who know you very well, what kind of professional position can they most easily see you performing well in. Pay close attention to their answers. If they see you doing something significantly different than what you are doing, consider making a change.

3. Make a list of the tasks you perform regularly that sap your energy. Find a way to delegate these to someone else.

4. Make a list of the tasks that energize you and that you could be performing more if you free up time by delegating those tasks you identified in question. Take steps to increase your time with these tasks.

CHAPTER THREE
BE GENEROUS WITH VALUE!

"Think of giving not as a duty but as a privilege."
-John D. Rockefeller Jr.

"We make a living by what we get, but we make a life by what we give."
- Winston Churchill

Movement in the traffic lane beside her brought Gus' attention back to the present. Hope of a break in the traffic was dashed when she realized that the movement was prompted by a gutsy but impatient traveler crossing the median to the other side in search of an alternate route. The momentary diversion over, Gus let her mind drift to another Baton Rouge businessman whose philosophy and business activities positioned him for financial success, as well for making a substantial contribution to the community.

Give Value Every Time

Michael Airhart states his philosophy very succinctly: "Givers Gain". Wikipedia says that **"Givers gain"** is the belief that when (business) people set goals to help others and honestly work to achieve these goals, they usually gained the most out of the experience – through a reciprocal benefit. It is also the strap line of BNI [Business Network International].

Though the internal value of "Givers Gain" was probably with him from childhood, Michael was introduced to the expression through his affiliation with one of the local BNI chapters. Gus recently overheard Michael talking to Marcy, a young mortgage lender who had asked him about his business practices. Marcy wanted to know how Michael had come to be so successful in an industry that was so competitive and had resulted in the implosion of many companies. She had recently visited the website http://ml-implode.com/ and was shocked at how many mortgage companies had crumpled under their own weight, many as victims of massive "sub-prime" lending schemes. How, Marcy wanted to know, had Louisiana Mortgage Lenders

(LML) escaped the fate that so many other companies, many older and larger than LML, had met.

When posed with the philosophy question, Mike responded, "It all comes back to Givers Gain. When you are making sure you are providing financial value and benefit to your customers and clients, the rest of it is going to take care of itself. You have to make sure you are giving the consumer value and communicating that value. If you show them the value of what you are providing to them, everything else will fall into place. Even if they don't accept your proposal at that time, they will often circle back to you sometime in the future."

Mike went on to share a story, which had been repeated several times over the history of his business. "About five years ago we worked with a gentleman who was buying a home. We worked closely with him, keeping him informed every step of the way and explaining what we were doing and why. He ended up rejecting our proposal and using another lender for that transaction. However, we stayed in touch with him, sending him our quarterly newsletter. Just last month he called us back. He said that he remembered how helpful and professional we were the last time. Naturally, our newsletter reminded him of that regularly. Now, five years later, he can't remember the name of the loan officer he worked with at the bank he chose at that time, but he remembers us. We have since successfully closed the loan with him, and he is a happy, and hopefully long term, customer. By giving him value regularly over the past five years, even when he wasn't yet a customer, we were able to bring him in. That's what I mean by 'Givers Gain'. "

Do the Right Thing

Her curiosity momentarily satisfied, Marcy excused herself and Gus took that opportunity to approach Mike.

"I couldn't help but overhear part of your conversation," she said to Mike. "I'm curious to know, if you had it to do all over again, what would you do differently?"

"That's a tough question," Mike laughed. "I'd have to give that some thought. But there are a few things I know I wouldn't change!"

"For instance?"

"For instance, our growth was slow and controlled. We have stayed the course through sixteen years in a tumultuous and ever changing industry. A lot of companies exploded overnight. We didn't ramp up rapidly and hire 300 people. That wasn't our business model. Then, when the economic and financial meltdown of 2008 and 2009 hit the industry, we did not implode either. We are still here and doing well. We came out of the timeframe all the better for having been small, nimble and able to adjust quickly to changing circumstances.

"Another," Mike continued, " is the 'Givers Gain' philosophy you heard me explaining earlier. People remember when you do the right thing. Also, we don't sell multiple financial products; we do one thing and do it well. We see time and time again that customers choose go to a bank, which sells many financial products. The bank employees are incentivized to up-sell and cross-sell. The customers often don't like that and the next time they have a need for a mortgage, they remember the advice and assistance we gave them, and they come back to us."

"Mike," Gus interjected, "I'd like to hear about the early days of your firm. What was that first year like?"

"It's funny," Mike mused. "Sometimes it feels like it was just yesterday and other times it was a lifetime ago…"

Louisiana Mortgage Lenders, LLC - Day One

A lot of important things happened on September 23, 1997: Mickey Rooney turned 77, Standard & Poor's upgraded Blue Cross/Blue Shield's rating went from BBB+ to A, and Louisiana Mortgage Lenders, L.L.C. was brought to life. At the tender age of 26, Michael Lee Airhart, along with a partner, leapt into the world of entrepreneurship.

Mike critiqued his reflection in the mirror as he prepared to leave home. Fresh haircut, white shirt, dark suit, red power tie... As he looked in the mirror, a mortgage broker looked back at him. Last week he was a well paid executive with a steady salary and as much security as working for someone else could provide. Today he was a self employed professional with all the potential and risk that went along with the title of Entrepreneur. Granted, he was an entrepreneur with no customers yet, but that would change. As Mike opened the door to his office that morning, he surveyed his surroundings, the tools of his trade: a desk, a chair, a computer and a telephone. He ignored the butterflies in his stomach and got to work. He knew what to do. His business plan had been established weeks ago, and his mind had been active. The cure for fear was the same as the cure for poverty: Activity. Not mindless activity though. Activity that was directed, sustained and well planned. Mike attacked that first day of his new venture with a ferocity born of optimism, determination and preparation. As it turned out, he was going to need all of the determination he could muster.

Mike and his partner joined forces and divided up the territory, with Mike taking East Baton Rouge Parish. With only one staff member between them, they began knocking on doors, leaping over many hurdles along the way. The first and most pressing issue was that of credibility in the marketplace. Potential customers wanted to know, "Who are you? How long have you been in business? Can you give some references? How about some testimonials?"

Giving Back to the Industry

As part of his quest to give back to the industry that had been good to him, and to be consistent with his philosophy of "Givers Gain", Mike had become involved with and donated a great deal of time to the mortgage lenders association. As a result of being associated with the organization that was widely viewed as working to improve the professionalism and reliability of the industry, Mike found that his own professional credibility was elevated.

Mike was very proud of the fact that Louisiana was one of the first states in the country to craft statewide legislation that created the mortgage loan officer license and that as part of his activities with the association, Mike was instrumental in drafting that legislation. Several years later in the 2009-2010 time frame following the 2008-2009 financial crisis, the National Organization of State Banking Regulators implemented a federal license that was patterned after the Louisiana license.

Clearly Mike's philosophy of "Giver's Gain" not only resulted in an improved business for himself but an improved industry for the state and then for the country.

Bright and early at 6:45 one Tuesday morning near

the end of the second year of his business, Mike was pulling up to the gates of the beautiful Country Club of Louisiana on Highland Road in South Baton Rouge, the meeting place of his BNI chapter. He was mulling over the events of the previous two years: interest rates had spiked in year one, his business partner had exited within twelve months, and he had made significant progress in overcoming the "stigma" of being a brand new company in an industry that values tradition and track record. All in all, it was a successful year and a testament to Mike's "Givers Gain" philosophy.

Companies can be Generous with Value

Gus was greatly relieved that the traffic finally broke and she was able to be on her way. She was headed to Shreveport to help her friend, FocalPoint Coach Karen Johnson, conduct a daylong retreat with a local company. The company was introducing all of its employees to DISC®, the assessment that had been so eye opening to Sherry Nivens.

The next morning was crisp and cold. Gus and Karen started their day sipping Karen's signature blend of coffee and chocolate while looking out the ceiling-high window of Karen's home, perched on Black Bayou in Benton, just north of Bossier City. They finalized their plans and estimated timings for the retreat and excitedly drove out to Los Paloma Sporting Range, deep in the woods North of Benton where the retreat was being held. The day was a rousing affair with a lot of good-natured ribbing and a plethora of "aha moments" where team members exclaimed, "So THAT's why you do that!" Watching groups of people begin the metamorphosis to a team never got old to Gus.

As they got in the car to begin the trek back, Karen asked Gus if she felt like going a little out of their way to meet a rising star in the aerosol business.

"Sure," Gus responded.

"Great, let's go to Minden!" Karen responded.

Gus was sure that they were going to be lost forever in the woods, but they finally found themselves on Highway 371 and, much to Gus's relief, saw the entrance ramp for Interstate 20 and soon afterwards the Minden exit.

"Help me watch for an eight-foot tall privacy fence. It will be on our left. It sort of blends in to the surroundings, and I usually miss it and have to turn around at the Dollar General.," Karen laughed.

Casey Rhymes - Rising Star

They found the eight-foot fence with no problems this time and, after stating their business at the call box, waited for the automated gate to lumber backwards to let them in. Gus gaped at the rows of tankers waiting to be dispatched not only to Aeropres' customers, but also to their customers' customers.

Karen followed the drive to a non-descript building, which housed the plant manager's office. While the atmosphere wasn't draconian, it certainly wasn't ostentatious. Gus searched for the word that best conveyed the feeling the plant gave her. The best one she could elicit was "utilitarian".

There was no receptionist at the desk when they let themselves in the glass door, so Karen led Gus a short trek down the hallway to Casey Rhyme's office. Casey was winding up a telephone call, so he gestured for Karen and Gus to settle into the two visitor's chairs in front of the desk. Gus was a little surprised at what she saw. Even though Karen had said Casey was a rising star, she still hadn't expected him to be so young! Karen had said that Casey had been with the company for 15 years. She hadn't expected to find someone who still qualified for the "40 under 40" award!

Casey replaced the receiver and stood to shake Gus' hand as Karen introduced them. His smile and warmth seemed to fill up the room. Karen commented, "That sounded like you were talking to a happy customer."

"Yes," Casey said. "Since oil prices are so low, we called their contract."

"You called their contract? That sounds bad!"

Casey chuckled, "It's not bad, I promise. Would you like me to explain?"

"Please do!"

Taking Care of Business by Taking Care of The Customer

"Here we are December and oil is trading at about $50 per barrel. Back in October, it was closer to $100. We don't trade oil, but the products we make are stripped from it. Therefore, the cost of making our products is directly affected by the price of oil.

"One of the products we buy is propane. We clean it up and then sell it to our aerosol customers. At the moment I can buy propane at about 50 cents per gallon when the norm was $1.00 back in October. Some of our bigger customers are on long-term contracts.

"Generally our larger customers prefer to have a contract price rather than to have to negotiate the price on every load. We send 5 or 6 truckloads a day to one of these companies! These contracts were locked in months ago when oil prices were significantly higher than they are now, at a rate that was favorable both to us and to our customers. We buy our propane on short-term contracts and then sell them on these long-term contracts.

"Our customers are aware, obviously, that our costs are directly tied to the cost of oil. They know that since our contract prices were agreed on when oil prices were at $100 per barrel, now that the price has dropped to $50 per barrel, we are making a huge margin. The 'pie' is only so big and basically in this industry, it's not getting any bigger. We want to split that pie so that everybody gets a piece, and everybody is successful. An adage I really like to use is that 'Pigs get fat: Hogs get slaughtered.' We don't want to be hogs.

"When we realized that the price of oil was becoming so volatile we called the contracts of our customers who purchase the lion's share of their aerosol from us. We let them know that we realize they are getting hammered right now. We set them up on a month-to-month contract until this energy situation stabilizes. They still don't have to recalculate the price on every load, and they get to share in the benefits of the lower cost of oil. When the time comes to lock in the long-term contract again, these customers are going to remember that we saved them substantial amounts of money that we didn't have to by doing this. We think they are more likely to be willing to negotiate a more favorable contract."

Gus was astounded at what she heard. "Can I ask a question Casey?"

"Sure."

"You saved your customer tons of money, but didn't that money essentially come out of your pocket? What did your CEO think about this?"

"We had an emergency meeting when all of this came up. Our CEO was a huge advocate of taking this action. We've done this in the past, and it has always worked out positively. Of course, we are here to make money and we have shareholders who are expecting us to make money. There are other places in the company where we are benefitting from the decreased oil prices, and we are not adjusting our rates. Furthermore, our smaller accounts aren't on long-term contracts so they are already getting the benefit of the low oil prices."

Customers Return the Favor

Karen interjected, "Has this ever gone the other way? Have you had to call your customers and ask to increase your prices because of an unexpected increase in the oil prices?"

"We've actually had some of these same customers call us and instigate the price increase. The aerosol industry is somewhat unique, and there are some great relationships there. We are in our 41st year of the business, and a lot of these companies have been our customers a long time and are longstanding friends of Aeropres. We are all trying to divide that pie fairly!"

Gus shook her head in wonderment. Recently, a survey was taken where researchers asked participants, "What is the first thing that comes to mind when you think of corporations?" The number one answer was "greed". Clearly those participants were not thinking of Aeropres.

Be Generous with Value!: Action Steps

1. Make a list of people who have helped you reach your current level of success. Write them a thank you note, or invite them to lunch so you can tell them how much you appreciate what they have done for you.

2. Look for opportunities to quietly bring your efforts on your customers' behalf to their attention. For example, if you are giving them a quantity discount, be sure to show that discount on the invoice.

3. Train your staff to make sure that every interaction you have with a customer would reflect well on you if it happened to make it the front page of the newspaper (or posted on their Facebook account).

CHAPTER FOUR
SUCCESS (OR LACK THEREOF) IS A RESULT OF YOUR CHOICES!

"Many of life's failures are people who did not realize how close they were to success when they gave up."
— Thomas A. Edison

"Some people succeed because they are destined to but most people succeed because they are determined to."
— Henry Ford

Gus waved a fond goodbye as she left Karen in Benton and headed South toward Baton Rouge. She was thinking about the Aeorpres philosophies and which of her clients she should share the story with. It was one of the best examples of a company looking after the best interests of their customers Gus had ever heard. She settled in for the four hour drive to Baton Rouge and turned the radio on just in time to hear the host of one of her favorite talk radio shows introduce his guest Joseph Facchiano. Gus had never met Joseph but had heard about him through some common friends. She turned the radio up.

Host: "Today we are going to be talking with Joseph Facchiano, and he's going to be talking about how success is choice: A proven plan for ensuring that you don't sabotage your own success. I'm sure there are people listening right now who have done this! We all do it to some degree. Now with over thirty years of experience throughout all areas of business, Joseph is a certified business performance coach, a keynote speaker, author and entrepreneur. Joseph has experience ranging from leadership and management information services in the apparel industry, to sales and sales management in telecommunications, to most recently, leading strategic data acquisition for Dun and Bradstreet. Joseph now shares his experience and business acumen with business owners, executives, hiring executives and students. Joseph's clients are business owners and professionals who have a track record of high performance in their lives and careers. They are highly motivated individuals capable of making the changes required to attain their goals and expect the highest quality of programs and support to help them get there. As business owners they recognize that their personal compensation is directly attributed to the quality of their skills, ongoing training and continual learning. They all recognize that they are capable of more... a LOT more. Considering that, I have to imagine that we are going to find some information today that no matter what you are doing, whether it is a small situation, or it's home (and you hear me say all the time that home is a business in itself), you will be able to pull some ideas, strategies and tips today from Joseph. So let me just say, 'Welcome Joseph!' "

Joseph (JF): "Thank you Tom, it's great to be here today."

Host: "You know the best thing about what we do here at Apex Radio and the experts that join us is that they all have walked their talk. It's not a bunch of people that have sat in seminars and read a bunch of books, and are just relaying the information to us. Why don't you just give us a little background? Tell us who you are, where you came from and exactly what it is you do."

JF: "Thanks Tom, and yes, I truly have journeyed this whole thing myself. One of the things one of my mentors, Brian Tracy, always tells me is that you can buy your experience or borrow it. I'm here to tell you that it's a lot easier to borrow it and learn from somebody else's mistakes than it is to make all those mistakes yourself. The stuff we are going to talk about today, I have been there. With thirty years in industry, like you said in the intro. In the apparel industry, I was in information technologies. I transitioned into a sales role in telecommunications and then later into more of a purchasing role with Dun and Bradstreet. Throughout it, what I learned is that the goals you set for yourself may sound great and may be 'SMART' goals, but there are a couple of things that you need to have lined up before you ever set your goals. This is what I truly learned the hard way, and that's why I want to share it with people today. I just learned that before you start setting goals for yourself, you need to have your house in order on these things."

Overcoming the Plateau

Host: "Along the way we've all experienced that sabotage, or that feeling stuck. You've obviously overcome that. Can you share a time when maybe you were stuck or sabotaging yourself before you learned how to overcome it?"

JF: "Sure. What I kept sensing throughout my career when I wanted to go on to the next level with my job. I looked up at management when I was an individual contributor. I felt that I wanted to lead this team, not just be a part of it. I always came up with these lofty goals, and then I would find myself being disappointed in one way or another. Sometimes you don't get what you wish for, and sometimes you DO get what you wish for, and it still isn't good. So I started to realize that there was something within me that was blocking my success, and I didn't know what it was. I had visions of myself going to a psychologist and having him say 'Yes, well, it's obvious that it's because your mother made you eat liver and onions when you were growing up, and that's the whole key to why your success is thwarted!' I had that scenario in my mind! I had the question of 'What is the barrier to my success, because there's got to be something there!' I wasn't setting goals to go to the moon. I was just trying to get to the next step in my career. Yet I knew that something was blocking me, and I just couldn't figure it out.

"Believe it or not, what I finally realized actually came out of what you would call a bad situation. Dun & Bradstreet eliminated my position. I had been tracking pretty well with them. I had had a several year career with them. I had different jobs with increasing responsibility, and I had moved up in the company. Everything seemed to be going pretty well. Then one day, I had put in my budget request for the coming year. When it came back marked up, I saw that what they had slashed happened to be my salary, so I knew what was coming.

"I made myself a promise the day that they told me that I had to leave Dun & Bradstreet: I would figure out why the Good Lord put me on this earth. I wasn't just going to go get another job. I was going to figure out what it is I was meant to do, and I was going to pursue that and ONLY that. It took a lot of discipline to do that...I had a family to support. I was basically saying that I have to get exactly what I want, or I'm not going to take it."

Joseph and Gus have Epiphanies

"During that process—epiphany if you will— it came to me that what I always wanted to do first and foremost was to be a coach and a mentor. No matter what my role or primary responsibility in my previous jobs had been, I always liked taking a high potential worker and helping that person achieve the next level."

At this point in the broadcast, Gus had to restrain herself from shouting "AMEN", because Joseph had just nailed the exact reason she had become a coach. She reached down and turned the volume just a little bit higher. A few less content commuters were expressing their opinions via their horns, and Gus didn't want to miss a word of what Joseph was saying.

JF: "I didn't put a lot of thought behind it. I just realized that that was what I truly wanted to do. So, imagine after thirty years, I find myself in this situation. For thirty years, I had worked and set goals for myself, and NOT ONCE, NOT EVER ONCE, was the goal that I was setting for myself totally aligned with what I truly loved to do! Now isn't THAT a smack in the head, right?!"

Host: "You had found your passion!"

JF: "Yeah! So I went about thinking, 'Why is this, and how could this have happened?' You know, we are all trained that if you are in a position and you do well, you will move to the next level. If you do even better you get to the NEXT level. And finally, I realized... that's just climbing stairs. That doesn't necessarily mean that you are ever really going to get to where you want to be... You are just trained that you are going to go up to the next step.

"So I pulled back from that, and I thought, 'I'm not that special of a person. I don't have unique problems. We all sort of fight the same battles in our lifetimes. So I figured if that was my "aha" moment, then there must be many people who experience the same thing.' In figuring that out, my mission was then clear. I was meant to help people achieve success. Not as it was defined by other people, but to help them define their own success and then achieve that!"

Success Means Helping Others

Host: "That's really noble. Most of us who have found some level of success have understood the principle that we are to share and support and guide others (By the way, I really love Brian Tracy). Whether it is a product that helps somebody's life or simply some information, we are all actually assisting other people while finding our own success! Right?"

JF: "Exactly! And I would go one step further and say that we will not get our own success unless we are in the mode of helping other people. That's a Zig Ziglar term, and it's true. You have to help other people achieve success in order for you to be successful yourself."

Host: "Right. We have to be of service in some way."

JF: "Truly, yes."

Host: "Joseph, you told me that you always like to present some 'power principles' whenever you speak. Can you share with everyone, what are 'power principles,' and share with us some you have prepared for today?"

JF: "That's great, Tom, and here you go, because you are going to keep one of the promises you made at the beginning of this discussion. You said to people that no matter what they do, they are going to get something out of this conversation that is going to help them. That's exactly what the power principles are. This is an idea I got directly from Brian Tracy (I would call myself a Brian Tracy disciple). Whenever we talk to people, whenever we coach or teach or mentor, we try to give everybody something that is going to help them in every area of their life. Not just how do I make better widgets, sell more of them, and make more profit. We really try to teach life lessons. So substitute 'life lessons' for 'power principles,' and you get what it is.

Are You a Victor or a Victim?

"Whenever I do speak with an audience, I always like to start with a few power principles. The first one I'd like to talk about today is the concept of VICTOR/VICTIM. Normally to do this, you have to have a white board and a couple of different color markers, but I can pretty much have the audience visualize VICTOR/VICTIM.

"Picture a line drawn across the middle of a page. That line is how we handle a challenge or a problem. When we talk about VICTOR/VICTIM, we are talking about behavior. What's your approach to a problem? How do you handle yourself, and how do you communicate with others in response to that problem?

You can either behave as a victor would behave, or you can behave as a victim. Below the 'problem' line, we have the victim behavior. If you use the acronym BENDS, you'll come up with some of the characteristics of victim behavior.

"Blame – When we are acting like a victim in response to a problem, we are trying to blame somebody else or place blame somewhere.

"Excuses – We try to come up with excuses as to why the problem happened. 'It's not anything that I did. The economy is bad… That's why it happened.'

"Negativity – Victims also display negative behaviors. They truly have a negative outlook. 'Oh we're doomed… we can't get past this.'

"Denial – If they don't have a negative attitude, they may deny the existence of the problem 'What problem…I don't see a problem here!'

"Scarcity – The scarcity principle is simply this: there's only so much good to go around. 'In order for me to get something good out of this problem, I'm sorry, but you have to lose. If I get a PLUS ONE then you have to get a MINUS ONE.'

"Now let's switch to the VICTOR Behavior. A victor says, 'It doesn't matter if I'm going to have one more piece of pie. Why don't we just go out and get a bigger pie. You don't have to lose in order for me to win. We can both win.' We refer to the victor's response to the problem as 'above the line'. The acronym is PROVE.

"Proactive – The victors are not reacting to problems all the time as much as seeing an opportunity to head a problem off before it becomes serious.

"Responsible- Victors are responsible. They are not looking to place blame, and they are not looking for excuses. They say, 'this is the problem. I am responsible. I've got it. I'll take care of it.'

"Optimistic- Victors believe that the problem can be solved. They believe that there is a better outlook after the problem is dealt with than there was before.

"Visionary – Victors foresee a day or a time when the problem no longer exists, and everything is better for having dealt with the problem.

"Enthusiastic – Victors approach each situation, good or bad, with enthusiasm.

"How does this apply to everyone? Victor/Victim is a choice. It is how you choose to react and what you choose your outlook to be in response to any problem. We can all, in any situation, decide if we are going to be victors or victims. We can get up in the morning and see burnt toast. The victor says, 'That's no problem; I'll just have an English muffin instead!' The victim can choose to say, 'Oh my gosh…I have burnt toast for breakfast. This is going to be a terrible day.' It's all our choice in how we deal with the problems that we are all going to face in life.

"The other key to Victor/Victim is quite simply this: If you understand it and you know it, you then have the chance to pull yourself out of victim behavior and get back up above to line to being a victor. If you understand it and you know, you also have the choice to help somebody else get themselves above the line before you have to deal with them. Victor/Victim is a very powerful principle because it basically says, 'Before we deal with this problem, let's make sure we are in the right frame of mind, that we have the right behaviors, and let's make sure the other person on the other side of the table is above that line too.' Because when everybody is above the line, things go a lot smoother. That's the first power principle, and that works everywhere in your life. You can see where that is not just a business issue."

Host: "That alone is worth the cost of admission! That alone can change lives, and it's like preaching to the choir, as they say. This is what I share with all my clients, and I have been blessed to work with people in forty countries. That sums it all up right there, Joseph. Einstein once said that when you change the way you look at something, what you look at changes. It means your perception is what changes. It's not what happens in life, but how you deal with it. If people will apply what you just shared, and were honest and truthful and aware, they would realize that their lives can change so much."

JF: "Absolutely."

Host: "Wayne Dyer once said about abundance…and abundance means financially, socially, personally, opportunities….if everyone took a trailer truck to the lake of abundance and filled it all day every day, it would never reduce the level in the lake of abundance. And that is what people don't understand when they are in the scarcity mindset. I think it is so cool that you put that in your power principle. If that alone is all that people take from this discussion, it can be revolutionary for them. I know this from experience, having come from literally nothing and growing up with very little, and being able to be successful. It came from applying what you just shared. When I changed the way I looked at things and stopped blaming and rationalizing, it all changed. So folks, please see the power in what was just shared with you."

Victors and Victims are That Way BY Choice

Gus took a moment to reflect on what she had just heard. Of course, she knew the VICTOR/VICTIM power principle. She had presented it many times in many different venues. However, just like her clients, she sometimes needed to be reminded that life is so much better when one is living above the line.

She glanced around at the faces of the drivers

around her, looking for indications of "Victors". Just a couple of cars ahead, Sherry Nivens seemed to be concentrating on something playing on her iPhone. She would listen intently, and then seemed to be speaking, rather haltingly. Gus was puzzled until she remembered Sherry saying that she was learning to speak Spanish so she could communicate with the natives on her next mission trip to Panama. Victor!

Gus heard some off-key singing and laughter, and glanced into the slightly battered Toyota Camry next to her. The young woman at the wheel was peering in the rear view mirror at her laughing child buckled into a car seat in the back. Both mother and child were singing at the top of their lungs and giggling uncontrollably. The traffic jam didn't seem to be hindering their determination to live above the line. Victors…definitely victors!

Gus wished she could say the same for the man in the shiny new forest green Jaguar XK Coupe with premium alloy wheels and the extremely loud horn. She couldn't help comparing the scowl on his face with the unfettered joy of the young woman in the battered Camry. This was a good reminder that the victim mindset can live in the souls of even the most gifted. He had chosen the victim mindset, and Gus briefly toyed with the idea of strolling back to his car and suggesting he turn on the radio program she was enjoying. Another glance at his countenance made her decide that her suggestion would not be accepted gracefully and she opted to stay in her car.

Gus turned her attention back to the radio program just in time to hear Joseph Facchiano responding to the host's request that he share his proven plan for assuring that he doesn't sabotage his own success.

We All Need SMART Goals

JF: "Let me first start out by saying…we all DO need goals. And they need to be SMART Goals…Specific, Measurable, Aligned with our Values, Realistic and Time bound. We need those in our lives. What I mean by sabotage is when we choose goals that are not aligned with our values. A lot of the people that I know set goals for themselves, myself included, never really stop to see if the goals we set are in alignment with our values.

"I came up with a process for determining Values, Vision and Mission before you ever set your goals. I found out a very amazing thing while going through this process. When you go through this process in the right order, and you are properly aligned with your values, then your goals become self evident. You don't have to sit around on New Year's Eve and say, 'What's going to be my resolution for the next year?' Because your goals are self evident and aligned with your true values, they become self fulfilling. That is what I have learned. Would you like to jump into the process now?"

Host: "Yes, Joseph. You mentioned Values, Vision, and Mission. How do you figure that out? How do people understand what that is?"

JF: "That's exactly what we are going to go into first. The process that I go through and I coach my clients through starts with, 'What are our values? What are the things we value'. Realize as we are going through this, we are not looking for the best sounding value. Values are very simple. They are personal. They are the things that when you see them, you like them. When you see them, you want more of those things in your life. Values are nouns. They are things. They are things that you appreciate and strive to attract more into your life.

"I am going to give you some examples of values, but remember… these are truly personal. What you like is what you like. You don't have to defend it to anyone, and you don't have to make sure it matches what anyone else likes. We were all given free will. Just as an example to put some values out there, I'm going to suggest some.

"Faith, Honor, Integrity, Family, Friends, Excellence, Professionalism, Philanthropy….

Values are Personal

"And one of my personal goals—I added this a little late in the deal—is a child's smile. I am a Junior Achievement volunteer, so I go into the classrooms and

I teach young children about business. You know, you look out across a class of thirty kids, and you don't really know who you are getting through to and who you are not reaching. One day, I went through a typical session, and at the end of the session, this beautiful young lady who wasn't really engaged in the prior sessions, smiled! When I left there I was walking on clouds. I said to myself, 'That's one of my values....I value a child's smile.' So I added it to my list.

"What are values? They are things that we like in our life, and we strive to have more of them. That sounds like a very basic thing, and it is basic. This is not quantum physics. Do I want the respect of people? Yes, I strive for that. Do I value my family and friends? Absolutely! I strive for that. One of the things I like personally is Excellence. I love Excellence in any form that I can get it. I watched the Olympics around the clock. I will watch obscure sports that I have no interest in at all...but to see the very best in the world doing what they do best, to me is a great joy. So I put *Excellence* on my list of values. I don't care if it is curling in the winter Olympics or rowing in the summer Olympics, to see the very best in the world doing what they do best gives me joy. I want more of that in my life, so I put it on my values list. Does that make sense?"

Host: "It's amazing! Everything you are saying makes me ask myself, 'Is he in my head?' I do the same thing. I couldn't care less about watching PGA golfers, but when Tiger Woods was really happening, I would watch just to see how good somebody could be at something. It just exhilarates me to watch anybody, whether they are dancers or figure skaters or whatever. Just to watch somebody be that good at something blows my mind, and it impresses me and brings up all those positive feelings. As we know, if you are in a positive mindset and a positive emotional place, then you will have outcomes that match. I am right with you!"

Value: Excellence

JF: "I will tell you a quick story about when I put EXCELLENCE on my list. By the way, let me stress that this isn't something you just sit down and put together, and you are done. You will add things to your list and reprioritize your list. There is no limit to how big your list can be or how small it can be. It's YOUR list.

"I remember the day that I added EXCELLENCE to my list of values. I was watching the ESPN classics when they had the biography of Secretariat, the horse, the Triple Crown Winner. In that biography, they showed Secretariat running the Belmont Stakes. I was only a teenager when this originally happened. I knew that somebody won the Triple Crown, but I had never really placed a high importance on it. It was great as a sports trivia question…no problem. But when I watched this horse run the Belmont Stakes, which is about a mile and a half, and he finished almost a quarter mile ahead of the second place horse...I looked at that and thought, 'I have never seen any athlete in any sport so magnificently outclass the field as in that one race!' I watched it, and I hit the DVR, and I watched it again. I was actually crying to see such magnificence! I'm not a horse racing fan. I watch the Kentucky Derby every year and that's it. But I remember watching that replay again and again, crying and saying..this is one of my values. I value Excellence! That is the day I put it on my list. It was so powerful!"

Host: "People may not understand the influence that has on you. It allows you to open the door and tap into your own brilliance and your own excellence."

JF: "Yes, you are right! You think, 'If somebody else (or some other animal can do it), why can't I?' "

Sherry Niven's Reaching for Excellence

Hearing Joseph Facchiano rave about excellence as a personal value and living "above the line" as a victor reminded Gus about watching Sherry Nivens the day before just a few yards away working toward becoming bilingual. Even though Sherry personified excellence, she would be the first to say that she was a work in progress, far from her own vision of "Excellent".

The two weeks between the "Know Yourself" and the "Know Your Business" coaching group meetings had been a whirlwind of activity for Sherry. Since Sherry was starting her business from scratch, she definitely felt a sense of urgency to get her marketing off the ground. She was also determined to market her practice in a manner that would reflect positively on her and the profession of which she was so proud.

The first step Sherry took was to establish a website, a Facebook page, and a Linked-In profile for her fledgling firm. Within hours of establishing her online presence, she got her first referral. Sherry was so engrossed in preparing for her upcoming "Classification Talk" scheduled for the next day's meeting at the Rotary Club of Mid City Baton Rouge that she was startled when her cell phone rang. "Sherry Nivens speaking….How can I help you?" she answered.

"Sherry, my name is Todd Larson," the voice on the other end began. "Cherie Barre suggested I give you a call. I own a small plumbing company and I think my business is in trouble, but I'm not sure. My bookkeeper gives me reports that I don't understand. All of our records are in *Fast-books* . She says I'm making a profit every month, but you can't tell it by the amount of money I have in the bank. Cherie says I can trust you and that you know what you are doing. Can you help me?"

Sherry felt a flutter of fear and elation at the same time. This kind of call was exactly why she had wanted to start her own firm. She had a passion for helping business owners who were struggling with understanding how to use their accounting systems as a tool for managing their businesses, and here was her very first opportunity to serve someone with exactly that need.

She put on her calmest and most professional voice. "Yes Mr. Larson, I'm sure I can help you. Would you like to come in to my office tomorrow at 3:00? Can you bring your last tax return and a backup copy of your accounting file?" She was gratified to hear the relief and hope in Todd's voice when he expressed his commitment to be there at the appointed time.

Unintended Consequences

As Sherry pressed "end" on her cell phone, she took a moment to reflect on the choices made that brought her to this moment in time. Sherry's formative years as a child were spent in Beauregard Parish in the small community of Sugartown. Her earliest memories include hours spent on the back of the family's Shetland pony, Jack, without benefit of bridle or saddle. One lazy afternoon Sherry ran crying to her mother claiming loudly that Jack had "bucked her off". Jean looked outside at Jack, head drooped…asleep… and concluded that Sherry had, once again, fallen asleep on Jack's back and tumbled to the ground. A piece of chocolate pie convinced Sherry that life was still good and that she should give Jack another chance.

In high school, Sherry began making choices that didn't seem monumental at the time, but ultimately paved the way to other opportunities and choices. East Beauregard High School was rather small and had relatively few options in the way of elective courses. In her senior year, Sherry found herself in a Physics class with three other seniors and a teacher who knew nothing about Physics. Mr. Arnold told them frankly in the first class that he knew nothing about the subject, had protested being assigned this class, and had no intention of teaching even the first lesson. As long as she showed up to class once in a while she was guaranteed an "A" on her transcript. Her classmates gladly took this opportunity to have a free hour, and many games of spades and poker were played.

Don't Take the Easy "A"

At the earliest opportunity, Christmas, Sherry transferred out of the "Guaranteed A" class into the bookkeeping class, taught by one of her favorite teachers, Barbara Hollier. Miss Hollier agreed to the switch, with the caveat that to get credit in the class Sherry had to successfully complete the "practice set" that was designed to take the entire school year. Sherry had only half the year to make this happen. Anything was better than facing another five months of boredom in the pseudo-physics class, so Sherry embraced the challenge.

Not only did she complete the practice set, with a 98% grade, she was the first in the class to be done. That seemingly small decision to leave the easy "A" in favor of a risky alternative set Sherry on a path toward her passion. She couldn't help but wonder, what would have been the outcome if she had taken the path of least resistance and stayed in the physics class?

Another decision that faced Sherry was the choice of colleges and majors. The major was a given: accounting. The choice of colleges…..not necessarily so easy. Ultimately in this case, Sherry did opt for the "easy" route. She was offered a full scholarship at McNeese State University in Lake Charles and she gladly accepted it. Her story was that she needed that scholarship, and that was why she chose McNeese. The REAL truth was that the thought of going to a large school far was just too terrifying. Sherry wanted to be able to go home whenever she felt the need, and McNeese was only sixty miles away. Still, the scholarship did come in handy!

Again, Sherry wondered how differently things would have been if she had opted for Louisiana's flagship university, LSU. As far as the quality of her education, Sherry felt that McNeese was excellent. In fact Sherry discovered later that the pass rate on the CPA exam was actually higher for McNeese than LSU. Sherry couldn't complain. She had passed the exam on her first try, and that was back in the day when candidates had to take all four parts at one time, on paper, and calculators weren't allowed!

Even so, now that she was in business for herself, Sherry was very aware that absolutely nobody cared what her GPA was or how high she scored on the CPA exam. What her clients, and potential clients, cared about was did they trust her, and did they like her. While the CPA certification was the entry level requirement, her network of friends and professional colleagues would make the difference in the success (failure was not an option) of her endeavor. It was slightly startling to Sherry to realize that if she had it to do all over again, she would study less, and socialize more (That's a little tidbit she couldn't imagine sharing with her daughter)! And if she had realized that she would make her professional life in Baton Rouge, she might have decided to attend LSU. But in all honesty, she couldn't say she was sorry that she went to McNeese, because it set the stage for her next decision that set her career on its current trajectory.

Random Choice with Far Reaching Consequences

By the time Sherry had reached her senior year at McNeese, she was sure of what she wanted to do. She wanted to work in public accounting and she wanted to go to new places and see new sights. So when a classmate invited her to make a trek over to San Antonio where she had a slate of interviews lined up, Sherry quickly agreed to tag along. It was her last semester, and she was bored with her classes and just couldn't wait to get to her "real life". Since Sherry didn't have interviews lined up she had to improvise.

Being young and a little naïve, Sherry didn't know that dropping in unannounced without an appointment with resume in hand is just "not done". So she did it. Another point she failed to take into consideration was that in the first quarter of the year (think tax season) every CPA firm was up to its eyeballs in work. This was definitely not the time to be trying to get an interview. Sherry didn't know she couldn't, so she did it. Sherry dropped in on every one of the "Big 6" international accounting firms in San Antonio. All but one of them refused to talk to her.

Big 6 Interview

To compound her audacity, Sherry showed up at the accounting firm's offices in the American Tower building in downtown San Antonio at 12:30. Predictably, the receptionist informed Sherry that the partner in charge of recruiting was at lunch. Sherry blithely said, "I'll wait," and made herself comfortable in one of the overstuffed chairs. Thinking back on that afternoon, Sherry realized the receptionist must have been new and didn't know how to handle this nervy young lady who had just set up camp in her lobby. Sherry heard her talking softly into the phone, hanging up and whispering into the receiver to someone who apparently agreed to rescue her from this interloper. In relieved gush, she exclaimed, "Mr. Buncomb will see you now."

A vertically challenged and horizontally gifted man with a mile wide grin and bubbling personality bounded into the reception area with the presence of a ringmaster ready to whip the crowd into a frenzy of excitement. He whisked Sherry back into his office with the enthusiasm rarely associated with members of the CPA community. It was months later when Sherry found out that Mr. Buncomb, Ted as he insisted she call him, was not the partner in charge of recruiting. Apparently he had consented to interviewing Sherry partly to calm the nerves of the frazzled receptionist, and partly as a welcome diversion from the tension inherent in the last two weeks of tax season.

A short time into the interview, Ted changed from light polite questions to more probing serious ones. Apparently he recognized that what he had before him was a diamond in the rough. Sherry never knew how much Ted had gone to bat for her. She never knew if it was because he always rooted for the underdog, or because he was impressed by her nerve and initiative. Maybe it was because she answered his questions with the confidence born of complete cluelessness that what she did was just "not done". Whatever it was, it worked. Sherry became the only member of her graduating class to snag an offer from one of the Big 6 accounting firms. Another seemingly innocuous choice, to go to San Antonio for a few days, ultimately resulted in a career opportunity that seemed totally out of reach just a short few weeks earlier.

Life is Full of Tough Choices

The morning after the trip to north Louisiana began for Gus in the same manner of most mornings, fighting the traffic and promising herself that one day she would begin each day on the beach sipping a libation with an umbrella. But in the mean time, there was work to be done. The snarling orange barrels apparently relaxed their iron grip on the unending line of cars, and with a minimum amount of residual frustration the last wave of intrepid commuters swept Gus on in to the parking lot of her office in the 7000 block of Jefferson Highway.

What once was a three bedroom, one bathroom

home had been converted to a warm, inviting, client-friendly space with real hardwood floors, high ceilings and soft soothing colors. Gus' only regret was that the fireplace was rendered inoperable. Gus made the choice to forgo the comforts of a wood burning fireplace partly due to the impracticality of maintaining a supply of firewood, and partly because the remodeling funds that had been allocated to the refurbishing of the chimney were used to remove the asbestos that made its unwelcome presence known soon after the remodeling commenced. "Oh well!" Gus sighed for the thousandth time. As Ursula the Sea Witch informed Ariel in Disney's *The Little Mermaid*, "Life is full of tough choices!"

Gus loved her office and held most of her one on one coaching session there. She rented conference room space from an executive suite downtown for her group sessions, but most of her work was done right here in these comfortable rooms. Her clients came here to let down their hair and bare their souls about their most pressing business challenges. Using time-tested techniques outlined in the coaching curriculum, Gus worked with clients on time management, team management, money management and exit strategies. Gus' clients have experienced business breakthroughs that have earned hundreds of thousands of dollars in addition to improved life balance. Gus often ruminated on how glad she was to have found her chosen field and wished for her clients the same level of overall satisfaction she experienced.

Jim Bridges' Tough Decision

Gus responded, "Come In!" to the soft knock on her door. "Oh," Marilly gushed as she opened the door. "I didn't realize you had come in. There is a gentleman here to see you. He says he has an appointment. His name is Jim Bridges, and he is a civil engineer. Isn't that funny... a civil engineer named Bridges?"

Gus chuckled, "Yes, I guess it is. Show him in."

Gus was pleasantly surprised to hear that Mr. Bridges had kept their appointment. He had won this coaching session at a silent auction conducted as a fundraiser by a local child advocacy organization. Twice before he had made the appointment only to cancel the day before saying he was just too busy to come.

Marilly ushered Mr. Bridges through the door setting his coffee on the conference table as Gus stood to shake his hand. His hand engulfed hers and seemed perfectly proportioned to his 6'4" frame. His head was shaved, his mustache and beard almost hid the fact that his smile was forced, and the dark circles under his eyes testified that his stated reason for cancelling his two previous appointments had probably been legitimate.

"Thank you for taking the time to see me Ms. Parker. I'm sorry I had to cancel our appointments before," Mr. Bridges opened.

"That's quite all right Mr. Bridges, and please, call me Gus."

"As long as you call me Jim."

"Agreed! Jim, when I conduct these complimentary sessions, I usually use a technique we call 'Diamond Mapping' out of the Clarity module in our coaching curriculum. But I suspect you have a particular issue you would like to address today. Am I correct?"

"As a matter of fact you are," Jim replied "I don't know what to do, and I hope you can tell me. There just aren't enough hours in the day to get everything done. I am working from 5:00 in the morning to 8:00 at night five days a week and eight hours on Saturdays, and I still can't catch up. Last Friday, my little girl had the lead role in her junior high play, and I missed it because I had to get a report finished to deliver to a client the next morning. The disappointment in her eyes the next day was just more than I could stand. I'm about ready to close the doors and just go get a job somewhere. At least then I would see more of my family."

"That's a pretty drastic step to take. Tell me a little more about your business. How long have you been in business...how many staff members you have....who your competitors are...who your clients are, etc.."

Ten Years and Bridges was Near Collapse

Gus settled in and listened intently as Jim poured out the ten-year history of his business. He relayed the familiar story often shared by the professional man or woman who grew tired of answering to someone else, all the while knowing that without their hard work, the boss would not have the big house in the Country Club and all of those great toys. She took a few notes while Jim reminisced about the first few lean years, and how excited he was to snare that big client that launched his firm into the arena playing with the "big boys". She sensed his distress mount as he told of accepting bigger and more challenging projects so that he could keep pace with his competitors. She heard the discouragement creep in as he told of holidays ignored and children's milestones missed as his work hours crept past reasonable to burdensome and now to onerous. She felt his despair as the kitten that was his business grew into a raging Bengal Tiger that owned him!

When he finished his story Gus was not surprised to see that Jim's eyes were shiny with unshed tears.

"So what do I do?" Jim whispered

"First I want you to recognize that you are not alone in this dilemma," Gus responded. "Countless other businesses have gotten their start exactly the same way yours did. Michael Gerber describes this in his book 'The E-Myth Revisited'. I strongly suggest you carve out some time to read this book. But first you have some decisions to make."

"What decisions?" Jim asked

"The first one is major," Gus replied. "You have to decide whether you want to stay in business for yourself. That decision drives all of the others."

"I don't know," Jim replied weakly. "I was hoping you could tell me if I should."

Gus responded kindly "If I could, I would, but that is something you have to do for yourself. I can help you with some techniques you can use to make that decision. And if you decide to keep your business, we can use coaching to help you bring this Tiger your business has become under control. Before we start, though, is there anyone else who has a vote in this decision. Your wife? A partner?"

"No," Jim assured Gus. "It's just me. I talked it over with Amaryllis before I came over this morning. She will support whatever decision I make. I used to talk all of these decisions over with my father, but he died two years ago. Now that I think about it, that's when things seemed to start spiraling out of control. My father was my confidant and my mentor. When I lost him, I lost the person I bounced ideas off of. I don't like to burden my wife with these things, and I can't tell my employees. My best friend works for one of my biggest clients so I certainly can't tell him that I don't know what to do! I feel like I've been drifting ever since I lost Dad.

You know, just saying all of this out loud has made me feel better than I've felt in months! Are you sure you aren't a therapist!"

Ben Franklin's Decision Making Model

"Positive!" Gus laughed. "Now I have an exercise for you. Don't worry. It's simple, but it is powerful. In fact, this is a technique similar to what Ben Franklin used to make decisions."

As she handed him a blank piece of paper and a pen, Gus instructed, "Draw a line down the center of the page. On the left side I want you write down all of the reasons you should keep your business. On the right side, I want you to list all the reasons to close it."

"Okay, when do you want this back?"

"Now."

"Now?"

"Now! I want you to do this right now. At the moment you are of two minds. You are remembering the good old days when you had a job where you only worked forty hours a week and had time with your family. At the same time you have enjoyed having your own business, making your own decisions and being master of your own fate. You came here this morning wishing that I could tell you what to do. Until you make this crucial decision, you are stuck. I will leave you alone for say, twenty minutes. I'm not saying you have to make your decision in that time frame, but you do need to identify the major pros and cons of each course of action. Can I get you another cup of coffee or a bottle of water to drink while you are thinking?"

"A bottle of water would be great," Jim responded with resignation.

Gus retrieved a cold bottle of water and left it with Jim as she softly closed the door behind her. She felt a little sorry for the panic in his eyes, but she knew this exercise was critical. Gus knew that If Jim didn't make this choice, circumstances would make it for him, and not necessarily to his liking. When she returned to the room twenty minutes later, Gus new from the change in his face that Jim had come to a decision. "So what did you decide?"

Success (or Lack Thereof) is a Result of Your Choices!: Action Steps

1. Write down at least five major goals. Make sure they are Specific, Measurable, in Alignment with your core values, Realistic and Time bound.

2. Find an accountability partner or coach with whom to share your goals.

3. Set up periodic meetings with your accountability partner to assess your progress toward your goals.

CHAPTER FIVE
CHOOSE WHO YOU LISTEN TO CAREFULLY!

"Be careful who you trust, the devil was once an angel."
— Ziad K. Abdelnour

"Trust is the glue of life. It's the most essential ingredient in effective communication. It's the foundational principle that holds all relationships."
— Stephen R. Covey

Later that day opening her mail, while sipping on a cup of Community Coffee's Bread Pudding single serving coffee, Gus found an invoice from her CPA, Pete Bratlie from Shreveport, LA. Gus had selected Pete to prepare her taxes after meeting him at a continuing education seminar sponsored by the

Society of Louisiana Certified Public Accountants. Over the course of the several months, Gus had discussions with Pete regarding his business philosophy. The most succinct way to express it is to "Render a Quality Service for a Reasonable Price". When asked how he makes sure he does that, Pete immediately replied that since it is his job to make sure that his clients pay the least amount of taxes possible, it is imperative that he stay on the cutting edge of the law. Pete quoted Judge Learned Hand reminding us, "Your obligation is to pay the least amount, not the most!"

Conventional Wisdom isn't Always Wise

A few months earlier in preparation for a speaking engagement, Gus had asked Pete to share some examples of "conventional wisdom" he had run across in his career that were just plain wrong. Pete shook his head in wonderment as he conveyed some of the vignettes that he and his colleagues had encountered during their years of serving the public.

"The most common misconception seems to be, 'I'm going to go into business so I can deduct everything.' You can deduct everything you spend for the business, certainly," Pete chuckled, "but being in business doesn't give you carte blanche to deduct EVERYTHING." Another common decision taxpayers often come to regret is buying rental property for the "deductions". Those who jump into rentals without consulting with an expert about their personal tax situations often find themselves on the unhappy side of Passive Activity Loss Limitations (If you don't know what this is PLEASE talk with your CPA before buying rental property!).

One of Pete's favorite stories that he tells often happened early in his career. One morning, he picked up the phone to hear one of his clients bark, "My brother-in-law said that if I buy diamonds, I can deduct them...Is that right?"

Pete paused and said, "No...Is your brother in law a CPA?"

"No," she responded.

Pete replied with probably the best advice he ever gave her: "Then don't listen to him!"

Pete shared a story of a time when his own firm did not listen to the experts and paid a heavy price for that choice. Back in the early 80's, Pete was with a firm that rented half of the ninth floor in the American Tower in downtown Shreveport. They were given an opportunity to move into a building in which the firm would be given an equity position for simply signing a lease. There was no equity at the outset, and it was easy to give away zero! The firm received equity equal to half of the space it would lease. Since the firm was leasing 55% of the building, it received 27.5% ownership of the building. Firm management approached the management of the

American Tower with the proposal that the Tower sublease their space. The firm offered to put up $5,000 to renovate the space for the new tenants. Tower management countered with the suggestion that the firm ante up $15,000. The firm balked and stood firmly on its offer of $5,000. The result…no sublease. The firm ended up having to pay for the unused space, at a total cost of about $75,000. Being an expert in taxes didn't make the firm an expert in real estate. The lesson….listen to the right expert.

Advice on Starting a Business

One of the most common situations Pete and his colleagues encounter is clients who want to start a business. Gus asked Pete how he answers when he is asked the question, "What do I need to know?" as he often is. Pete explained that there are a myriad of things that business owners, both new and 'seasoned', need to know and do in order to be profitable and to be able to keep the majority of that profit. It is unlikely that any one person will have all of the answers to all of the questions. In fact, most people are not aware of all of the questions they need to ask. Because of this, Pete explained, he always advises potential business owners to select four people that they can rely on for professional advice and guidance:

1. A banker
2. A lawyer
3. An Insurance Agent
4. A CPA

"Five," Gus interjected. "They also need a coach."

"Er...so sorry...Five. I appreciate that. Once those people are lined up the prospective business owner can go out and do what he does best. His professional team will be there to answer those specific questions as the needs arise.

Pete went on to say that it is imperative that the prospective business owners accurately estimate the expenses they will incur and how much revenue they will be able to generate to cover them. A source of cash to make up the difference is critical. Many potential businesses have died on the vine because their founders were too optimistic in their estimations of revenue and unrealistic in their projections of expenses. In his many years of working with businesses, only a handful were profitable right away, and of those, only one was in the black in the first month. Most businesses take several months, or even years, to reach that point.

Hindsight is 20/20

Pete's observations brought to mind a conversation Gus had had with Richard Young of Young Equipment Solutions Inc. of Shreveport, LA. Richard embarked in the food service equipment industry in 1977 with Frymaster Corporation. In Richard's words, "It was a beginning of a wonderful adventure!" His adventures with Frymaster and subsequent companies took him all over the world and moved him and his family to multiple locations in the United States. In the early 2000s, family obligations compelled him to return to his home of Shreveport. With a quarter century of food service equipment industry experience behind him, Richard thought he would retire. He thought wrong!

Less than a year into his "retirement", Richard received a call from an old friend in the industry who said, "You need to start a manufacturer's representative business." Richard, who had already begun to realize that retirement was not his calling, reflected on the fact that he knew most of the major players in the industry. There is a joke in the industry that once you get into the food service equipment business, you can't get out. The only way to leave the industry is to die. Since Richard wasn't ready to die, it did not take him long to decide to jump back in and see what would happen.

On December 16, 2002, Young Equipment Solutions, Inc. was born. Richard and his partner in Tennessee began reaching out to their industry contacts and within a year had a respectable book of business to show for their efforts. On day one of the business, the staffing and equipment consisted of Richard, a laptop computer and a cell phone. By 2004 they were on the map, representing some of the best manufacturers in the business. In the course of three years, the business had grown to five employees, strategically placed throughout their territory of Louisiana, Mississippi, Arkansas and Tennessee. By the company's fourteenth birthday, it was doing millions of dollars in sales, resulting in hundreds of thousands of dollars in commission revenue.

Gus had asked Richard the question that often makes entrepreneurs turn slightly green, "If you had known then what you know now, what would you have done differently?"

With a contemplative expression, Richard responded, "I would have spent more time with my CPA and would have set up our compensation much differently. For starters, I would have brought my wife into the business as an employee. She had quit work many years ago when our second child was born and therefore did not accumulate the 40 quarters needed to qualify for social security benefits. She could have helped me quite a bit and been paid accordingly.

"During the first several years of the business, I did not take a salary from the business and paid a lot of my travel expenses personally. If had set a salary for myself during those lean years, the amount due could have built up as a debt, and then I could have taken the funds out later when the business could afford it." Echoing Pete Bratlie, Richard continued, "I would advise anyone starting a business, with all of the complications in the laws these days, consult with an attorney and a CPA to see how to best set up your business."

Gus resisted the urge to remind him that a Business Coach wouldn't hurt either!

Choose Who You Listen To Carefully!: Action Steps

1. Set up a meeting at least semi-annually to discuss your business with your CPA. Make sure he knows changes you have made or are considering making so he can advise you as to the tax implications.

2. Have an independent insurance agent review your coverage. Make absolutely sure you are covered for all the ways and places you do business. An insurance friend of mine once told me about performing a review on a business that sold most of its products overseas. He found that the company's general liability coverage did not cover overseas activities. Don't be that guy!

3. Get a business coach.

CHAPTER SIX
ASK FOR WHAT YOU WANT!

"Ask for what you want and be prepared to get it!"
— *Maya Angelou*

"Ask with Confidence, listen with humility."
— *Charlie Van Hecke, The Art of the Q: Build Your Business with Questions*

Gus turned her thoughts to a recent lively conversation with Sherry Nivens and Pete Bratlie. As a member of one of the committees for the Society of Louisiana CPAs, Pete Bratlie often found himself passing through Baton Rouge on his way to the Big Easy. At Gus' request, he stopped in for dinner with Sherry and Gus in order to share with Sherry some of the wisdom he had gained from thirty plus years in public accounting, including stints as employer, employee, partner and rainmaker. Gus and Sherry were already seated at Gus's favorite table at P.F. Chang's when Pete arrived. They had agreed on an early dinner, as Pete still had a little over an hour of driving ahead of him.

How To Get Referrals

Sherry was anxious to hear what Pete had to say and barely let him get settled before she fired off her first question. It was rather predictable…"How do you get clients?"

Pete smiled and pointed out that more important than clients are "great clients". "A great client would be defined as someone who asks your advice, pays your bill and refers people to you. The part that gets skipped most of the time is the referral. Word of mouth is what typically builds CPA firms, as it has mine, but that seems to be the part that is the hardest to make happen. Asking for my advice and paying my bill will make you a 'good client'. The often missing link to being a great client is sending referrals."

Gus interjected, "Pete, how do you go about asking for referrals?"

"Well," he responded, " I let people know that I am open for business!" Pete went on to tell about a seminar he had attended years ago. The presenter, a CPA from Australia, was a real cheerleader who had built and sold three CPA firms in California. There is a four letter word that CPAs should never use. That word is spelled B-U-S-Y! If someone asks you what's going on, and you respond that you are busier than a one-armed paper hanger, that person is not going to send you more business. He is going to think that you aren't going to be able to take care of them! A better response is, "Business is great and I'm looking for more!"

Just that morning Pete had experienced a similar situation. He was going up the escalator to the second floor of the Shreveport Convention Center, where his Rotary Club meeting was just about to start. He caught the eye of an Edward Jones representative who was on the down escalator. She inquired, "Are things getting busy for you?"

Pete replied, "Well, we have a few things that have come in already, and there's always room for more."

She turned around, looked up and said "I'm glad to know that". The four letter word (busy) was not used, and the door was opened for referrals.

Over the years, Pete has developed a reputation and relationship with attorneys, many in the Shreveport area. Some came from referrals from other attorneys and others because he 'button holed' them. Pete reminisced about an attorney who was a racquetball partner, but not a client. One day while they were playing racquetball at the downtown YMCA, the attorney asked Pete, "How much would you charge me to do my tax return?"

Pete quickly responded with a very low dollar amount. The attorney let the ball whiz by him, sure that he had misheard. "Wait, no, that can't be right." Pete smiled and assured the man that that was his price for attorneys who send him business. "I have a little corporation. How much do you charge for that?" the attorney asked quizzically. The same amount was Pete's reply. Since the attorney had been paying about four times that amount, he made an immediate switch.

A couple of years later the attorney had become lax about sending the referrals. Pete sent him a short note reminding him that the bargain rate required action on the attorney's part in the form of referrals. Within a couple of days, the referrals started again. <u>Sometimes you have to ask for what you want more than once!</u>

<u>Dan Creed's Champions Network</u>

Sherry left that dinner with her head reeling. Could it really be as simple as that? Just ask? The next morning Sherry called Gus. "Gus, when I left last night, I thought it sounded too easy to just ask. Now that I've thought about it, it sounds too hard. It seems a little rude to just outright ask people for referrals. I know Pete felt comfortable asking his racquetball partner, but I just can't see me doing that. Besides, I don't play racquetball!" she whined mournfully.

Gus laughed cheerfully at Sherry's woeful sound. "Don't worry, Sherry. We have a system, and I will be glad to show it to you. In fact, at our next coaching group meeting, Working Your Champion's Network is going to be our topic. It's really going to be a game changer."

"What is a champion's network? And whatever it is, I don't have one!" Sherry complained.

"Yes you do. You just don't know it yet. Let me summarize it for you. Dan Creed, also known as 'Mr. Lucky', coined that phrase. Dan is a FocalPoint Business coach in Arizona and is the unprecedented six-time winner of the Brian Tracy Award of Excellence/Coach of The Year for FocalPoint Coaching International and the 2010 winner of FocalPoint Coaching Practice of the Year.

"Sherry, you are ready for this. With the other members of the group, you have worked hard to identify exactly what service you are providing to your clients. You've determined who your ideal client is. You've even done the research to find out where your ideal clients are likely to work, play and worship. Now it's time for you to build up and activate your network.

"The first thing I want you to do is to make a massive list of everybody you know or THINK you know. Once you've made the list, I want to you break it down into classes. Class A consists of people you are already doing business with or who are already referring business to you. Class B is made of folks who, with a little bit of grooming, probably would do business with you or send you referrals. Class C is everybody else who likes you, but does not fit into Class A or B. Does that make sense?"

"I guess so," Sherry replied. "What do I do after I make the list?"

"That's easy," Gus replied. "You are going to start contacting them. You are going to let them know what you are doing and offer to help them in any way you can. You are going to ask them how you can refer business to them. You are going to become a RESOURCE to them. Sherry, have you ever heard of the 'Law of Reciprocity'?"

"No, I don't think I have."

The Law of Reciprocity

"Even if you haven't heard of it, you've probably experienced it. The Law of Reciprocity basically says that one good turn deserves another. If you do something nice for someone else, they want to do something nice back for you. And it really doesn't matter that much whether they like you. For example, if you were to buy lunch for a co-worker and soon afterwards ask that person to buy some candy from your daughter's school fund raiser, there is a good chance that the co-worker will buy more candy than he would have if you had not bought him lunch. In fact, he might buy enough candy to more than cover the cost of the lunch you bought."

"How does that affect me and my champions list?" Sherry wondered out loud.

"For starters, you are going to make a point to provide something of value to your champions," Gus asserted.

"Gus, I'm working on a shoestring here. I can't afford to go out and buy gifts for everybody I know. Besides, that seems a little cheesy to send them a gift and say, 'Oh by the way, give me the names and phone numbers of five of your friends!' "

Gus laughed, "I agree, that IS cheesy. Fortunately, that is not at all what I am proposing. For starters, an item of value doesn't have to cost anything. Have you ever seen an article in a magazine or on the internet and thought of someone who would really like it, or would be helped by it?"

"Of course."

"Okay, how many times did you cut out that article or forward that link to the person you thought of?"

"Um....never."

"That article is an item of value, and it doesn't have to cost you anything. It tells that person that you value him or her enough that you are thinking about them when you aren't with them. It also tells them that they are important enough to you that you took your valuable time to send them the item. You've just made a deposit into that relationship bank. You've given them a reason to think of you when they otherwise wouldn't have.

"Let's take this scenario a little bit further. Let's say that right after they opened that link and ready that funny, useful or interesting story you sent them, that a friend of theirs walks into their office, plops down on their visitor's chair and says......I need a new CPA!. Who is your champion going to think of first?"

"Me!"

"Bingo...You! Now clearly that is a simplified example and it will probably take more than one touch to keep you on the top of your champion's mind. That is why you need to have a system in place to consistently reach out to your champions. You will also want to reach out in different ways. Sometimes it will be a telephone call, sometimes dropping in just to say hello...you might even see something going on that you want to take a picture of and text to them. It just depends on where their interests lie and exactly how close to them you already are. You will also need to be sure not to reach out too often, especially if they aren't reaching back. You don't want to come across as a stalker."

Working Your Champions List

"If I spend time looking for items of value and

making phone calls and texts to everybody I know, when am I going to work?" Sherry asked.

"Good question, I'm glad you brought that up. Remember I said that you would classify them A, B and C?"

"Yes."

"You will have more frequent contacts with the A's than the B's. Likewise, the C's will get the least attention. Also, based on their reactions and reciprocations to your outreach, some of your contacts will change classifications. A 'B' who sends you a referral immediately becomes an 'A', and you will spend more time and effort keeping close contact with him.

"Now let me ask you a question, Sherry. What is the item of most value you can send to a champion?"

"Oh, I know the answer to that one. It's the same thing I want.... a referral!"

"Absolutely! I recommend that as soon as you give your champion's contact information to someone, that you call your champion to give him as much information on the referral as you can. This way, even if the person doesn't act on it, your champion knows that you have been trying to send him business. You could go one step further and ask that person if it is okay to have your champion call her. That way your champion can initiate the contact and have a better chance of closing the deal. A good referral is the absolute best 'item of value' you can send to one of your champions."

"So, do I keep track of the referrals I send?" Sherry queried.

"No. It might seem a little counterintuitive, but you really have to approach this with a mindset of being willing to give without expectation of receiving. Even though ultimately you know you are going to receive. I know it sounds a little strange, and I'm not going all mystical on you, but as the old saying goes 'what goes around, comes around'. If you start sending good referrals, ultimately you'll start getting them back, and it might not be from the same people you send them to. When you start getting the reputation of being an Uber-referrer, other professionals are likely to start sending referrals to you in hopes of getting on your radar."

"You mean I would be someone else's champion?" Sherry trilled.

"You probably already are!"

Tracking the Touches

"I still think it's going to be pretty hard to keep up with who, when, and how often I've 'touched' people. I assume you have a system for keeping track. Do you just set up tasks in Outlook, or keep an Excel spreadsheet? What do you do?"

"You could do those things," Gus replied. "In fact, I tried the Excel spreadsheet route at the beginning of my practice. What I found was that first of all, I really didn't have a good idea of how often I needed to be reaching out to the different classes of champions. Then I was constantly forgetting to add to my spreadsheet when I reached out and whether I connected. It just turned out to be a big mess. Don't tell anybody, but I almost threw up my hand in disgust and blew off the whole idea. Fortunately my coach let me in on his secret of how he kept on top of all of his 'touches'."

"YOU have a coach?" Sherry exclaimed in amazement.

"Of course I do. Why does that surprise you?"

"I thought coaches were only for people who are struggling like me."

"On the contrary, coaching is for high performers. Sherry, your struggles are due to the stage your business is in, not because you are a poor performer. I only work with professionals who have high potential. Didn't you know that?"

"No, I thought you just felt sorry for me."

Gus laughed. "Not in the least. Now let's get back on topic. Carlos told me about a service called Refer.com. Their website is www.Refer.com. It is a cloud-based service. You put your contacts in and rank them as we discussed. Then refer will send you a notification of who is 'due' for what kind of 'touch'. Then once I make the touch, I mark it as "done" in Refer and put notes in my CRM. It's pretty simple. Both Refer and my CRM have apps, so I can do all the record keeping on my iPad. It beats the heck out of a spreadsheet. My friend Karen Johnson in Shreveport likes Refer.com so much that she has an affiliate link on her website."

"Speaking of being on topic, remind me again how this is going to get referrals for me."

"It's going to get referrals for you because as you reach out and 'touch' the people in your champions network, you are going to become a resource for them. You are going to work on becoming their 'go to' person whenever they need something, even if it has nothing to do with your profession. Then, when the time comes for you to ask for a referral, they are going to want to bend over backwards to say yes!"

"That sounds awesome! I'm going to check out that website and choose a CRM system!" Sherry replied. "I'll see you at group!"

Gus hung up the phone duly impressed with Sherry's enthusiasm. "She really is a high performer," Gus thought, "and a pleasure to coach!"

Ask for what you Want!: Action Items

1. Compile your list of champions following the instructions Gus gave to Sherry.

2. Implement your system for tracking touches and get started today making the first touch.

3. If your position includes sales or client development of any type, select and implement a CRM system as soon as possible.

CHAPTER SEVEN
CHOOSE YOUR PARTNERS CAREFULLY!

"It is rare to find a business partner who is selfless. If you are lucky it happens once in a lifetime."
-Michael Eisner

"If you like a person you say 'let's go into business together.' Man is a social animal after all. But such partnerships are fraught with danger."
-Brian Tracy

Earlier in the week, Gus had the opportunity to have a brief conversation with Jake Netterville, former Chairman of the American Institute of Certified Public Accountants and former Managing Partner of Postlethwaite & Netterville. Gus had been duly impressed when reading the details on the history of Jake's firm on their website, www.pncpa.com. The firm had spawned not one but TWO AICPA chairmen, garnered a trainload of business accolades, and had grown from a single shingle firm, established by Alexander Postlethwaite in 1949, to one of the top accounting firms in the nation.

When a man enjoying the reputation, credentials and business savvy like Jake Netterville speaks, the wise person listens! Gus had asked Jake what was the biggest challenge he had overcome to reach the phenomenal success to this point in his career. At that question Jake had to chuckle and replied, "Anytime you are in a partnership with more than one person, yourself, you've got problems! I often said during the time I was managing partner, it's like being married to more than one woman. Each of the partners has different desires, qualities and faults, as we all do. To be able to bring that group together to form consensus on anything we chose to do was always difficult."

Gus had to concur. In her "previous life" as a CPA in public practice, she had encountered a myriad of partnership situations…none of them ideal!

Opposites Attract

We've all heard the old adage "Opposites Attract". This is true….and it isn't. Opposites in communication styles and personality as well as approaches to challenges and dealing with people…those are some opposites that can make for a very healthy, well-managed and potentially successful partnership. But when the "Opposites" are in values and ethics, the outcomes aren't so wonderful.

<u>When it's true…</u>

Imagine if you will…(insert "Twilight Zone" music here) a partnership where each partner was a hard-driving, fast-talking visionary who could make a decision at the drop of a hat, and change directions suddenly and without warning. Can you imagine that partnership creating a vision, working toward that vision and meeting with a great deal of success? On the contrary, it's much easier to imagine that partnership ending up as a train wreck.

Let's take the same partnership and assume one of the partners kept that previously described pattern of behavior. Let's make the other partner more careful about changing directions, more likely to think through the consequences of changing direction, less interested in being the center of attention and more likely to attend to the details of implementing the vision. Now we have a partnership that has a better chance of setting the world on fire instead of crashing and burning.

Well then, one might think, let's just dispose of the

first partner altogether. Obviously she is loud, flighty and slightly obnoxious. Without her, however, the vision is limited, and the more careful partner might never get started. No…both personalities can make a critical contribution to the success of the partnership.

When it Isn't…..

The area in which opposites not only don't attract, but actually repel is in the area of core values. A person's core values are those characteristics or beliefs that are so deeply held that they are inseparable from their being. Without adherence to these values, the person would be unable to function. When the core values of the partners are not at least compatible, a functional partnership is virtually impossible.

Hard Times at 'Small Times'

In the late nineties, a young woman we'll call Kristy came to Gus, who was at the time practicing as a CPA. Kristy planned to open a daycare center in a small town just outside of New Orleans. Since this was an endeavor that was too big for her to tackle alone, Kristy had recruited her husband's cousin to be her partner.

By this time, Gus had seen enough bad endings to have some standing advice for people who were considering a partnership, especially with family…

"Don't!". But if you insist in going into a partnership, at least make sure you have a written partnership agreement outlining the expectations, responsibilities and duties of each partner, and spelling out the circumstances under which the partnership could be dissolved. Unfortunately, Kristy did not follow any of this advice. With a great deal of excitement, Kristy and Janine opened *Small Times* in a building that was purchased via a bank loan signed only by Kristy and her husband, George. Within a few months the excitement began to turn to disappointment, irritation, and finally anger and bitterness.

The first sign of the clash of core values came within the first month. One beautiful Friday morning, tired because of the late hours she had spent updating the accounting records on Thursday night, Kristy was chagrined to pull up into the parking lot at *Small Times* and see two employees and several parents, with tots in tow, waiting outside the locked door. What??? It was Janine's day to open the center, but she was nowhere in sight. As she dashed to the door frantically searching for her keys in her purse, Kristy apologized profusely to the visibly irritated parents.

Once the children, who were no worse for the wear, were settled into their routines, and the ruffled parents were soothed and sent on their way, Kristy reached for her phone to call Janine's home. There must have been some crisis, and Kristy's mind filled with dark visions of car wrecks, heart attacks, tornadoes, typhoons…since that was the type of event that would be necessary to make her fail to open the center on time…right? Wrong! After the fifth ring, Kristy heard a sleepy "hello?" Janine had overslept, and Kristy was stunned.

As she quietly placed the receiver on the cradle, she could hear her father's voice saying, "Your word is your bond. Always do what you say you will do." Clearly Janine did not hold that same value.

If that had been the only conflict in values, the partnership might have survived, or even thrived. Alas, it was just the beginning of a painful and conflict-ridden year.

Frightening Fridays

Fridays proved to be the day of the week most likely to bring out the differences between the core values held by Kristy and Janine. A few weeks after the late opening incident, Kristy asked Janine to make some time to discuss their division of duties. Janine had been in charge of hiring and supervising the direct care workers and preparing snacks and meals for the children. Consequently, she felt that her obligations were met and her day was over at 3:30 when the 3 year olds had finished their snacks. By 3:45, Janine was hurrying home to cook dinner for her three teenage boys and however many of their friends showed up!

Janine's house was "the place to be" for many of the kids on the high school baseball team. Her sons Luke and Carson made up the dynamic pitcher/catcher combination that had catapulted the team to the championship playoffs for the last three years. This was Luke's senior year, and Janine was determined to spend as much time with him as possible. She knew that next fall meant Luke would be changing his address to a dorm room. She hoped it would be LSU, but knew that he had his eye on those "other" Tigers, Clemson. Janine sometimes looked in on the boys after they had gone to sleep at night, looking for signs of the little league boys who used to sleep in those rooms. She marveled at how the time had flown and how little of it was left.

Some Issues Call for More Than a Discussion

Janine was a little antsy at 3:45 when Kristy finally got off the phone with the bank. Kristy has asked Janine to stay a little later than normal to talk for a few minutes, and now she was already ten minutes late leaving. She knew the boys would be famished when they stormed in after baseball practice. Kristy cleared her throat and started off as she had practiced. She had read several management books and knew that she had to keep the tone positive and non-accusatory. She had to use those

"I" statements and make sure she didn't put Janine on the spot...at least not too much.

"Janine. You, Um.. I mean , I need some help. You might not realize it, but I have been here working until at least 6:00 every evening and sometimes until 7:00. When we started this, I had no idea how much paperwork was involved. Now that we have the Class A license, the paperwork is even more important and more tedious. The reports we have to submit to the state are horrendous, but we have to do them since over half of our clients qualify for state assistance. Without these students, we wouldn't be eking out the small profit that we are making, so letting them go is not really an option."

Janine relaxed a bit. So this is what was up. Kristy had been complaining about how hard she was working lately, so this meeting finally made sense! "I know what you mean," Janine commiserated. "I've been having a hard time getting out of here on time lately myself. I hear what you are saying, and I agree!"

"You do?" Kristy exclaimed, relieved.

"Absolutely! I think we need to hire somebody as soon as possible, and I have just the person. Darlene Pritchard mentioned at the game last week that she just got laid off. I think she was a bookkeeper, or something like that. She can come in at 3:00 to help me get the kitchen cleaned up and then stay to help you do those reports. This is perfect!"

"No," Kristy sighed. "This is not perfect. That's not what I'm saying at all. We can't afford to hire anyone. We just aren't making enough profit yet. What I was getting at is that I would like you to take over preparing the child nutrition reports that have to go to the state, as well as the ordering of the food. I calculated that this is taking me about 6 - 8 hours per week. If you take them over, we could both leave by 5:00 most days."

Janine was silent for a long thirty seconds and then answered with a quiver in her voice. "Kristy, I hate to say this, but I just can't help you. I told you when you asked me to be a part of this that I would not sacrifice my family time. It's not my fault you miscalculated how time consuming the reports are. The boys have already made comments about how I'm sometimes late for their games. If I stay until 5:00 every day, I would be neglecting my family, and I'm not willing to do that. You will have to find another way." With that Janine hurried out of the building. Her "family first" value had just collided head on with Kristy's "high work ethic" value, and both parties felt abused and unappreciated.

Clash of Core Values

Gus wished she could say that this was the end of the clash of the values, but it wasn't. As time went on, Janine found that Kristy was, in her mind, a little too stingy with the children. Janine had always been told that she was "generous to a fault", and Kristy had a way of making her feel like it was an actual character flaw.

After their conversation about Janine taking on some additional duties, she had started ordering the kitchen supplies, including the food. Every time Kristy saw the resulting bills, she had a comment to make about how much "unnecessary" money she was spending. Couldn't she see that the small treats were the only luxuries some of these children would get? Most of the children lived in a single parent home, and those hard working mothers just couldn't provide some of the extras. Janine felt like that was part of the reason she was in this business. If she couldn't provide a little bit of extra happiness to these boys and girls, what was the point of being here in the first place? Janine's core value of "generosity" was taking a serious toll on Kristy's core value of "frugality".

The battle of conflicting values went on until finally, just after the one year anniversary of the opening of *Small Times,* Kristy and Janine parted ways. Besides losing a partner, Kristy had lost a friend and created tension in the extended family. Neither woman had a "bad" set of values, but their values just weren't compatible.

But …How do you KNOW?

"How do you know if our personalities and values

will mesh"? This time Kristy was asking the questions before entering into another partnership. By this time Gus had relinquished her CPA practice and was focusing all of her professional efforts in coaching high performing individuals. This was Kristy's first coaching session, and she was bringing Gus up to speed on what had happened at *Small Times*.

"That is an excellent question," Gus replied. "The short answer is the long answer: time. Spend time with your potential partner in many different circumstances. See her when she is not feeling her best or is not consciously on her best behavior. See how she handles the situation when the airline loses her luggage or cancels her flight. Watch how she treats the waiters at a restaurant she frequents often, and one where she never expects to come back. These situations can give you a hint as to her behavioral styles as well as her core values."

"Aren't there any short cuts?" Kristy begged.

"I don't know if I would call it a short cut, but I do have a couple of tools for you," Gus laughed.

"What is it? I'll take it!" Kristy had been looking for a partner to pick up the slack Janine left when she abandoned the partnership. She had found someone who appeared to be perfect, but after her experience with Janine, she was much more cautious about binding herself to someone.

"One is an assessment of each of your intrinsic

motivators and, the other is called a DISC® assessment."

"DISK? I have a daycare, not a farm," Kristy replied, puzzled.

"No, It's DISC® D –I- S- C. In fact, it is one of the first things you will be doing as part of the coaching process. The DISC® assessment will help us determine what your preferred communication and behavioral styles are. I can do a better job of coaching you when I understand your preferred styles. I recommend you have Susan take one as well. When the two of you discuss and understand your natural communications styles, you improve your chances of effectively communicating with each other," Gus explained.

"So this will tell me if Susan has the same work ethic and what did you call them…core values… I have," Kristy asked.

"The DISC® identifies communication and behavioral styles, not values or skills. It will, however, be a great start in determining how well you are likely to work together. The motivator report will help you determine if the same kinds of things are important to you. This will help each of you to know in what type of environment each of you thrive. Then you can figure out between you if you can make the environment at the center fit the requirements."

During the next few coaching sessions, Kristy came up with a plan that seemed to work well. She hired

Susan as Assistant Manager with specific duties, including the responsibility of ordering the kitchen supplies and keeping the meal cost per child within pre-established parameters. Over the next several months, she included Susan in the coaching sessions, during which they, as a team, worked out the key performance indicators for the business, as well as strategies for attracting their ideal clients.

After a year of working together, and getting to know each other very well, Susan and Kristy agreed that partnership was a viable option. *SmallTimes* was making a big splash in Washington Parish. The right partner made all the difference!

Choose your Partners Carefully! Action Steps

1. If you have a written partnership agreement with all duties and expectations spelled out, pat yourself on the back. Work together to create a list of the core values of the organization.

2. If you are already in a partnership and do not have a written document with all the duties and expectations written out, draw one up as soon as possible. See Action Step #1. Discuss it with your partner while you are still 'friends'. Have it reviewed by an attorney who is familiar with the pitfalls common in your parish/county/state/country.

If you are in discussions with someone about becoming partners refer to Action Steps #1 and #2. Have this in writing before you sign on the dotted line, or put any money into the partnership.

CHAPTER EIGHT
WORK HARD!

"Good things aren't supposed to just fall into your lap. God is very generous, but He expects you to do your part first."
- Audrey Hepburn

"There's only one growth strategy: work hard."
- William Hague

Gus glanced at her iPhone and realized that she had better get herself in gear! An old friend, Hardy Foreman, was coming to town, and Gus was looking forward to some pleasant conversation. Hardy had recently completed a stint as President for the Shreveport Chapter of the Louisiana Society of CPAs and was presently serving as a Member-At-Large of the Board of Directors for the Louisiana Society of CPAs.

Knowing that Baton Rouge traffic had become her personal nemesis, Gus wanted to leave her office early to ensure she had ample time to reach Mike Anderson's Restaurant before Hardy arrived. She had promised him a great seafood lunch, since those were hard to come by in his native Shreveport, and she knew Mike Anderson's would fit the bill.

Hardy Foreman, CPA

Hardy graduated from Louisiana State University – Shreveport with a Bachelors Degree in Accounting in 1999. He started his career at a large local firm in Shreveport and stayed with them over four years. This firm had paid for his last two years of college through a scholarship. His professors, demonstrating again that his philosophy of hard work paid dividends, had nominated him for the scholarship. Even though he wasn't legally or even ethically required to work for them, he felt there was a moral debt. Nearly five years of hard work seemed to be sufficient to satisfy that debt, and while he had enjoyed the time tremendously, he knew it was time to move on.

The local firm happened to be in the same building as KPMG, one of the world's largest International CPA firms. Hardy had turned down an offer from KPMG in favor of the local firm right after graduation. Being the friendly, open person that he is, Hardy got to know some of the KPMG staff members and learned more about their firm. He discovered that KPMG provided world-class training to their team members, and he wanted that! In a move that was atypical for the industry, Hardy moved from a local firm to a "Big 5" International firm.

His year at KPMG brought "hard work" to a whole new level. Hardy had recently gotten married, and the all-night stints at his desk didn't fit well with the responsibilities of a new husband. So after about a year, Hardy tried the "industry" route. He worked in a small family business with a group of people he enjoyed tremendously. However, over time he realized that if you pointed out a particular day of the month, he could tell you exactly what he would be doing that day. The repetition and predictability had his "hard work gene" in a chokehold. In another non-traditional career move, Hardy went back to public accounting!

Hardy subsequently moved to a smaller CPA firm where he was on the partner track. The partnership position materialized almost simultaneously with the firm's acquisition by Carr Riggs and Ingram, CPAs and Advisors. CRI was the 27th largest firm in the United States at the time of the acquisition and was steadily moving up that ladder.

Be The Hardest Working Guy In the Room

Hardy breezed in the front door of the iconic restaurant looking crisp and cool in his sharply creased khaki pants and his Carr Riggs and Ingram polo shirt. His normal attire was the "CPA uniform", suit and tie, but today was a travel day so he had dressed down. His eyes searched the bar area just inside the front door until they landed on Gus in the back corner, and a smile took over his face. As he slid into the booth opposite Gus, he reminded Gus of her promise to provide delicious seafood.

"I've been thinking about what you asked me," Hardy commented.

"What did I ask you, and when?" Gus responded quizzically.

"At the Controller's workshop last spring when you were speaking on Time Management, we were talking at the break. You asked me what my business philosophy was, but they called us back into the session before I got a chance to answer. I thought about it on the way down here, and if you are still interested, I'd be glad to share it with you."

"By all means, I'm still interested, and I'd like to hear it."

"It's really pretty simple. Our objective at Carr Riggs and Ingram, fits with what my goal has been from the very beginning of my career. And that is to provide the best client service of any professional service firm in our area. My philosophy is to surround myself with the good quality people who are 'client centered'. I hire them and groom them to be the best possible supporting cast. Every day I strive to be the best CPA that I can be, and I surround myself with people who share that philosophy. If we are all doing what we can to improve every day, then we can do the best possible job for our clients. We might not be the brightest and we might not be the best, but as long as we keep our focus on the client and strive to be better, then we will achieve our goal of the best professional service for our clients."

Gus smiled and said, "Since you are the brightest and you are the best, then that's not very hard to do, is it?"

"I'm not going to say that," Hardy humbly responded. "But I am the hardest working. I've always said that someone might be smarter than me, and they might be better than me, but they will never outwork me."

"I don't how familiar you are with different CPA firms, but before the Enron debacle, Arthur Andersen was the 'gold standard' in our profession. I read a book about the culture at Arthur Andersen and learned an amazing fact about them. They were the only firm in the 'big five' that grew totally organically. All the other firms achieved their enormity of size and gained their place in the "big five" through mergers. Arthur Andersen never merged with another firm.

"I believe the reason they were so successful was the way they recruited staff members. They would look at the 'A' students, but would not necessarily consider them to be top candidates. They looked for students who had good, but not perfect, grades. They looked for the student who had worked throughout his/her college career. Arthur Andersen wanted the candidates who were aggressive 'go-getters' who worked, who participated in extracurricular activities and who had internships. They would take the student with a 3.5 GPA and a full time job over the guy with a 4.0 who never had to juggle competing priorities. They didn't want the girl who only had to go to class, study and sleep. They wanted that blue-collar work ethic.

"Growing up in a life of privilege didn't seem to be the proper preparation for being successful at Arthur Andersen. Arthur Andersen's approach of building their business with this core group of people proves that you don't have to be the best and brightest. You just have to outwork the ones who are."

Relationships are Key

"That sounds like a very reasonable approach, Hardy. How has that played out for you?"

"I really like working with family-owned businesses, in part because you can get the decision makers all in one room and come to resolutions. I have a special place in my heart for working with relatively small family-owned businesses. I have acquired most of my book of business through relationships and referrals.

"I am the CPA for the majority of the local agents of a national insurance company. It started with one agent. She was very happy with my work, and referred me to another agent, who then referred me to another one. It just grew from that. Several of the agents that I work with are responsible for training other agents. So, when there is a new agent coming up through the ranks, they will spend time with one of these agents who I already work with. When their discussion comes around to accounting, they will often say, 'This is Hardy. He's my CPA. He should be yours too!'

"To make this happen, I had to have a strong team in place with team members who are dedicated to delivering what we promise. That strong work ethic is critical. My team has consistently given our clients a product that we can be proud of and that the clients are pleased with."

"I see how finding the right team members who each have a strong work ethic and business philosophy like yours has been instrumental in your success. However, I keep hearing from my clients that those people just aren't out there. How do you find them, and can I share your secret with my clients?" queried Gus.

"It's funny," Hardy smiled, "again, it's through

relationships. One of our best sources for finding people who will fit into our culture is our current staff. When someone on our staff tells us, 'Hey, I know this guy who would be the ideal candidate,' we take a serious look at him. Our team members know what we want and need for our team, and they know which of their friends and acquaintances will fit in.

"There is no doubt that it is hard to find good people in our profession. This is one of the reasons we chose to merge with CRI. We have increased our access to good people. No matter what the topic is, CRI has an expert in that field somewhere in the system. We no longer have to limit our pool of expertise to only those people in the Shreveport area."

Gus thought back to an earlier conversation she had had with Hardy when she asked him why he had chosen accounting in general as his career and public accounting in particular. Hardy gave credit to a very wise advisor at LSU-S, Janie Slusher. Hardy was forward thinking enough, even as a young man, to know that he had to have a degree that would prepare him for a career which would allow him to be self-supporting and find his own way. Hardy came from that blue-collar, hard-working, down-to-earth background that he ultimately learned to value in his team members. He knew he wanted to major in business, and beyond that he was open to suggestions.

Ms. Slusher's suggestion of Accounting was right

on target. She pointed out to Hardy that Accounting was the only business degree that would allow him to pick which area of business he wanted to stay in. The others, such as finance, marketing and management, would lock him in to a career path upon graduation. An accounting degree opened up options.

Accounting is Tough!

Many business majors will tell you that Accounting was the second hardest subject they had to master (statistics being the hardest). When Hardy reach the 200 level courses in the accounting curriculum, he saw many of his classmates struggling mightily with the courses that he found to be relatively easy. That natural aptitude for accounting coupled with his propensity for hard work positioned him to excel in his chosen field.

At the time Hardy graduated to become licensed as a Certified Public Accountant, candidates were required to work at least two years in public accounting, in addition to passing a massive examination. While some people liken the world of public accounting to the worst kind of hell, Hardy excelled. He found it to be a profession that above all else rewarded hard work. He recognized that it wasn't easy, and every day he was doing something different. Hardy quickly found that he liked the challenge and the variety. In summary, public accounting was a field that rewarded hard work. And

Hardy excelled in working hard.

The waitress delivered two platters of some of the best shrimp, crawfish and scallops Baton Rouge had to offer. Neither Gus nor Hardy found they had to work hard to enjoy their lunch!

<u>Work Hard!: Action Steps</u>

1. Be brutally honest with yourself. Look back at the last week at work and estimate the number of hours you "wasted". If you don't think you were ever unproductive, try this exercise. Get a blank sheet of paper and draw a line down the middle. Head up one column as "productive" and the other as "wasted". Set a timer to go off every 15 minutes. When your timer sounds, put a hash mark in the appropriate column for how you have spent the last 15 minutes. If your time was wasted, write down what you were doing that was wasteful. Do this for three days and start making the appropriate changes in your habits.

2. Resolve to wake up a half hour earlier and get to the office a half an hour earlier and make use of that time. If getting there earlier is simply not an option, then stay a half hour later. You'll probably make up most of that time by reducing the amount of time you sit in traffic.

CHAPTER NINE
CHOOSE YOUR TEAM MEMBERS CAREFULLY!

"The way a team plays as a whole determines its success. You may have the greatest bunch of individual stars in the world, but if they don't play together, the club won't be worth a dime."
— *Babe Ruth*

"Trust but Verify."
-- *Ronald Reagan*

The next morning, as Gus pulled into the parking lot at the YMCA heading for her personal "Battle of the Bulge", she reflected on the conversation with Hardy. While he heartily espoused his belief in hard work, his actions and statements demonstrated another belief, the necessity of a strong team. Regardless of how good, how smart, how motivated, or how hard a person works, success is unlikely without a strong team.

Years of experiences, both good and bad, had left Gus with a four word philosophy regarding team members: Hire character, teach skills. She thought back to a "Ted Talk" she frequently reviews during which Simon Sinek says, "If you hire people just because they can do the job they'll work for your money, but if you hire someone who believes what you believe they will work with you with blood, sweat and tears."

Dave Ramsey, in his book "EntreLeadership", defined employees as someone who "comes to work late, leaves early and steals while they are there." Dave cautions that business owners need "Team Members", not "Employees". Gus couldn't agree more!

When Team Members Rebel

As she stepped onto the treadmill for her warm-up, Gus spied Bart Hatfield across the room. Bart owned and managed a very successful sign and print company. A couple of years ago, Bart found himself in a difficult situation with one of the team members responsible for installing the signs the company produced.

A local television station had requested the company to create and install some full color graphics in an area that would sometimes be included in the shots on the air. Proper preparation and installation were critical to this project. Bart reviewed the area and concluded that the job was definitely within their scope of expertise and promptly sent the installer, Jim Dodd, out to review the proposed worksite. Much to Bart's surprise, Jim returned to the shop shaking his head.

"What's wrong, Jim?" Bart asked.

"It's too dangerous! We can't do the job," Jim replied. "The desks I would have to stand on won't support my weight. I am not going to do it."

Jim had been with Bart for many years, and had never before refused to do a job. Wondering if he had missed something, Bart went back to the television station and pored over the job area again. He even went as far as jumping up and down on the maligned desks. Bart had to be sure that he was not letting the fact that this was a slow period and the revenue from this job would be very timely hold sway over his judgment.

Bart concluded that the job was indeed doable and could be done safely. He confronted the reluctant Jim and insisted that he go back out and reevaluate the scene. After acknowledging the client's willingness to remove some screens that could have caused a hazard, and that all of the employees would vacate the area during the entire installation process, Jim grudgingly agreed that the job was doable.

Since Jim had been a long term valuable member of the team and had previously demonstrated his commitment to the team, Bart gave his concerns and opinions adequate consideration. Unknown to Jim, Bart had decided that if Jim came back from his second visit still insisting that the job was too dangerous, they would turn it down. It would hurt the revenue in the short run, but in the long run Bart felt it was more important to support his team. Forcing Jim to participate in an installation he felt was unsafe could only cause trouble in the future. Bart's response of treating his team member with consideration and respect resulted in a continued working relationship, a stronger team, and fortunately a nice revenue boost during a slow period.

When Employees Use Their Creativity Against You

As Gus stepped onto the dreaded treadmill her thoughts turned to other examples of when employees were less than ethical in carrying out their assigned duties. She had scanned a recent report from the Association of Certified Fraud Examiners (ACFE.com) where she was startled to learn that each year a typical business loses about 5% of their revenues to fraud. For the year being reported, that translated into a global loss of almost $4 trillion. Gus had spewed her coffee back into the cup when she saw that number! 4 Trillion…..with a "T"….Trillion! A stack of four trillion one-dollar bills would go to the moon and back SEVERAL TIMES! When placed in that perspective, it almost made the incidents she knew about almost seem small, even though no theft or fraud is small to the victim.

The foundation of any relationship is trust. Without trust in your prospective spouse, you don't marry. Without trust in your teenager, you don't loan your car. Without trust in your bookkeeper, you don't turn over all of the accounts receivable, accounts payable, general ledger and banking duties. Without trust….the bookkeeper can't steal you blind. For the first time in a long time, Gus thought about a story she had read in the local newspaper about a small company that had fallen victim to excessive trust and inadequate monitoring.

But I Trusted Her…She Used to Babysit my Kids!

Joyce (not her real name) had worked for Redd Rivers Construction (not the company's real name) since high school. She started out helping Mrs. Redd in the office after school. On Saturday evenings, she stayed with Samuel and Shaun while Mr. and Mrs. Redd (Virginia and Tom) enjoyed a well deserved date night.

After graduation from South Street High School, Joyce continued her education at Clarke County Community College, completing a two-year degree in accounting and finishing in the top quarter of the class. She paid for her education through student loans and working for Redd Rivers Construction, first part-time and then full-time. It was a heavy load, but at the time, Joyce was certain the accounting degree was the key to her leaving this one-horse town.

As the business grew, Virginia came to rely more and more on Joyce. Mr. Redd's reputation for excellent work along with his effusive personality brought them so much business that it generated almost more paperwork than the two ladies could keep up with. To complicate bookkeeping matters, Virginia had taken to traveling with Tom as he ventured into other parts of the country to monitor job sites and place new bids. For all practical purposes Joyce was handling everything, all by herself. "You would think," she complained often to her husband, "if I'm going to do the work of two people that they would pay me both salaries!"

One Monday morning, Virginia rushed into the office slightly breathless. "Joyce, Tom got a call last night from the plant manager at the Pennsylvania job. There is a small problem with the job and a big problem with the customer. We are leaving this afternoon to see if we can smooth things over. Will you be okay with everything here?"

"Mrs. Redd, payroll is due Thursday, and you are the only one with administrator level access."

Virginia stopped and scribbled a few letters and numbers on a scratch pad. "Here are the access codes. If you have any problems running the payroll, call Cindy at the CPA's office. She can help you. Don't you use the same software down at the church?"

"Yes ma'am. I've prepared the payroll there a couple of times when the treasurer was on vacation. I'm sure it will be fine."

"Thanks Joyce. I don't know what we would do without you. You are a godsend!"

Unanticipated Resentment

As Joyce watched Mrs. Redd rush from the office and settle into her new Champagne colored Lexus sedan, she caught sight of her own ten-year-old trusty Toyota Corolla. It occurred to her just then that she was still driving the car her father had given her as a gift at her high school graduation. She smiled at the memory of how thrilled her father was to provide his only daughter with such an extravagant gift. At the time Redd Rivers Construction was just getting off the ground and Mrs. Redd was driving a slightly battered but still respectable Toyota Avalon.

Her smile faded as she realized that in the ensuing decade, Mrs. Redd had treated herself to a new and better car about every three years, with the Lexus being the most recent and most luxurious. Not only that, Sam and Shaun, both now attending college at Louisiana Tech, were sharing a Toyota 4-Runner that was half the age of the Corolla of which her father had been so proud.

As Joyce compared her situation to that of her employer, she couldn't help feeling resentful. While Mr. and Mrs. Redd's income had increased exponentially, her own income had not come even close to keeping pace. In the past she really hadn't noticed it because the money her husband Mark made working in the oilfield kept them and their sons Nathan and Nick comfortable. In fact, they had planned to buy Joyce a new car this fall. They had even picked out the one she wanted. It was a certified pre-owned Toyota Camry - Baby Blue with only 45,000 miles and a sunroof!

But that was before Mark lost his job. It seems all of the oil drilling had moved up north. Several of Mark's buddies had moved to Pennsylvania following the work, but Mark didn't want to leave their home. It just wasn't fair! When the work moved away, Mark wasn't able to replace it locally. The Redd's just went to where the money was and never missed a payday. It just wasn't fair!

Find the Bleeding

Several months later, Tom and Virginia Redd sat on their back patio sipping their morning coffee and looking out over the placid lake they had come to love. They had bought the home eight years ago, not because the house was so desirable, but because they wanted their boys to have the opportunity to make all the memories that having a lake as their back yard could provide. Six months after moving in, they realized that their boys were wholly unimpressed with the lake, but Tom and Virginia were hooked!

"What's on your mind, Tom?" Virginia asked. Tom had been unusually quiet this morning, and in retrospect Virginia realized he had seemed preoccupied for the last several days.

"Do you remember that PetroPlant job I told you about a few weeks ago?" Tom responded.

"Sure!" Virginia said. "Didn't you say it is the biggest job you've ever done, and the profit on it should be almost as much as we made all year last year?"

"That's the one," Tom acknowledged. "They've put it on hold. We will still do the job, but the start date has been pushed back six months. And they aren't the only one. The low price on natural gas has caused three other projects to be put on hold."

"Should I be concerned? Do we need to downsize to a smaller house?" Virginia asked worriedly.

"No, but we are going to have to tighten our belts. I'd like you to help me look for areas we can save money in the company. Even with this downturn, it just seems like we aren't making as much as we should be. We are bleeding money somewhere. I'd like you to look at the jobs we've done this past year and see where we need to apply a tourniquet."

Red Flags Everywhere

The next day was Saturday, so Virginia decided to take advantage of the quiet time in the office to start looking for the answers Tom so desperately needed. Virginia sat at her desk and looked around for the letter opener to open the mail. Not finding it, she went to Joyce's area and opened the desk drawer in search of the elusive implement.

To Virginia's surprise, right next to the letter opener, was a ring with a stone that looked to be about half a carat in size. *Surely that's not a real diamond*, Virginia thought. Unless they struck oil on the Sanders' homestead, there is no way Joyce could afford a real diamond that big. And if she did surely she wouldn't be careless enough to leave it at the office!

Virginia pushed the thought of the diamond aside and settled down at her desk to go through the mail. She was upset to find several past due notices from some of their biggest vendors. The most alarming item was a notice from the Internal Revenue Service with a penalty for late payroll taxes. How can this be? Where was all of their cash going?

Virginia turned to her computer. It was time to get to the bottom of this! She put the administrator password into the system and waited while the hourglass turned summersaults. When she got the message "Access Denied", she decided it was time for a manicure. Obviously her nails were too long and were causing her to make keyboarding errors. Virginia carefully reentered the password she knew by heart. Again, "Access Denied".

Puzzled, Virginia picked up the office phone and called Joyce. After two rings, she heard a tentative "Hello?" on the other end.

"Joyce, this is Virginia. I'm trying to get into the accounting system, and my password is not working. Did you change it?"

"What are you doing that for?" Joyce asked in a tone that seemed strange to Virginia.

"Joyce, I'm just catching up on a few items, and I need the password. What is it?"

"Virginia, I'll be happy to take care of whatever needs to be done. If you'll just leave me a list, I'll get to it first thing Monday morning. In fact, come to think of it, I could use a break from the kids. I'll come right now."

"No Joyce!" Virginia said a little more harsh than she meant to. "I do not want you to come in. I just want you to give me the password."

After a short pause and a long sigh Joyce said, "Itsmine."

"Actually Joyce, it's my password. I'm the administrator and you have your own sign on," Virginia replied, slightly confused.

"That's the password," Joyce said resignedly. "I T S M I N E. All capital letters."

"I see," said Virginia, with a growing sense of dread settling in the bottom of her stomach. The thought of that ring flashed through her mind again, but she refused to dwell on it. She was just being silly! Joyce had been with them for ten years and for goodness sakes, she had baby-sat the boys. Joyce would never do anything like that.

With a bit more effort this time, Virginia pushed those niggling doubts back down next to the knot in the pit of her stomach and returned to her task.

The Ugly Truth

With the accounting system password successfully entered, Virginia began her review by running a report of all the income and expenses charged to each of the jobs conducted in the last six months. *This is strange*, she thought. *According to the job income and expense report, we lost money on the ChemCentral Plant job and I remember Tom being particularly pleased with that job because there were no weather delays and he didn't even have to work the crews on overtime. We should have made a nice profit on it.*

As Virginia dug into the details of the ChemCentral Plant Job and several others in the past year, she vacillated between shock, denial and overwhelming grief. It had started small. The first irregularity she stumbled upon was an extra paycheck for Joyce. The really strange part was that the paycheck was charged to the

Pennsylvania Plant job. Virginia vaguely remembered giving Joyce the administrator password and payroll pin as she rushed out the door to join Tom on the trip to smooth the ruffled feathers of that very important client.

As Virginia continued to dig, she finally had to admit that what she believed was impossible was staring her in the face. With a lump in her throat she reached for her cell phone to call Tom. What made Virginia the angriest is that she was having to be the one to break this news to Tom. This was going to break his heart. He had always felt protective of Joyce, and had looked at her as a member of the family. What Virginia was about to say would color every good memory they had ever shared with Joyce. How could Virginia tell Tom that in the last six months alone, Joyce had stolen more money than they had profited?

Virginia walked back to Joyce's desk and opened the drawer. She looked for the engraved CZ that would tell her the stone was a Cubic Zirconium. It wasn't there. Finally, she took off her own ring, a beautiful two-carat diamond solitaire that had been part of her grandmother's estate. With her hands trembling, Virginia held both rings up to her quivering lips and blew. Neither ring fogged. It was a real diamond.

Joyce's subsequent arrest was the subject of many a lunchtime gabfest, but it barely merited a mention in the news. The local television station reported that a local bookkeeper had been arrested and charged with embezzlement. The newspaper had not even mentioned it. It wasn't a newsworthy event, but it changed the lives of Tom and Virginia Redd. They had trusted too much, monitored too little and had been betrayed.

Choose your Team Members Carefully!: Action Steps

1. Review your operation systems to identify areas of risk. Consider having an outside professional perform the review. Implement controls over these areas.

2. Familiarize yourself with common red flags that could indicate an employee is stealing.

3. If you believe you have found an instance of employee theft, contact your attorney and follow her guidance on how to gather evidence and when to report the theft to authorities. Be sure you are right and that you have proof.

CHAPTER TEN
CHOOSE YOUR CUSTOMERS CAREFULLY!

"For there to be betrayal, there would have to have been trust first."
- Suzanne Collins, The Hunger Games

If it seems to good to be true, it probably is.

Gus waived to Bart as he left the cardio room and remembered some funny (or not so funny really!) stories he had shared during the social time at a networking group meeting. Bart had recently celebrated his 20th anniversary of his franchise. Throughout those years he had learned the hard way that sometimes certain customers were more trouble than they were worth.

The Customer Who Can't Be Pleased

Bart told the story of the Nguyen couple who owned a nail shop near his College Drive location. On one occasion, Mrs. Nguyen came into the shop and ordered a sign. She approved all the specs, graphics and materials, then authorized the final drawing. The order was placed, and work began on the sign.

A couple of days later, Bart knew trouble was brewing when he saw the couple come into the store. Mr. Nguyen burst through the door like a man on a mission, and his wife slipped in quietly behind him. Mr. Nguyen did not like the sign! In a show of good faith, Bart remade the sign at no charge.

A few weeks later Mrs. Nguyen came in again. Bart tactfully questioned her on whether Mr. Nguyen would be happy with the results. She assured Bart that Mr. Nguyen would like it. The order was placed. The scene was repeated. Again, Bart remade the sign.

Hoping that the third time would be the charm, when Mrs. Nguyen came in again Bart gave it one more try. One more time he ended up remaking a sign at no charge. When Mr. Nguyen came into to pick up the revised sign, Bart invited him to find another printer. As a wise man once said, "Go down the street and put somebody else out of business!"

The Customer Who Doesn't Honor His Promises

Mr. Nguyen wasn't the only customer who had caused Bart come consternation! In the early nineties, before cell phones became the ubiquitous extension of our persons, Bart found himself the unwilling holder of some rather pricey signs that had been specially ordered and fully approved by a local outdoor entertainment company. Message after message was left for the owner imploring him to pick up his signs.

Since this was not the first time this exact sign had been ordered, Bart had not felt it was necessary to secure a deposit from this customer, so he was in danger of losing money on this job if he couldn't persuade the customer to pick up, and pay for, these signs. After three attempts at having the customer come in, being a man of action, Bart decided to toss the signs in the back of his car and head over to the customer's office to bring the transaction, and his frustration with it, to a close. That is not exactly how it turned out!

Bart arrived at the customer's location, nonchalantly walked in the front door, and asked for the owner, Mr. Flamenco, who was conveniently "on his way to the bank but would be right back". Bart declined to identify himself, hoping to not put the personnel on notice that he was there to collect a debt. He waited quietly in the lobby, refraining from engaging in chit chat, not wanting his distinctive voice to give away his identity. Anonymity was critical to his mission.

The Key Incident

Along with being a man of action, Bart was a man of measured caution, and therefore routinely locked his car upon exiting. It was with great chagrin that he realized his keys had not accompanied him into the building. Now he was in a conundrum. His only hope for getting back into his car without having to sacrifice a window was to call his wife to bring the extra set. He couldn't call his wife without using the customer's phone. His customer was in a freestanding building with no adjoining businesses that he could discretely visit to borrow a telephone. Walking half a mile in the Louisiana heat did not appeal to Bart in the least! What to do? What to do? He made the call and in doing so, alerted the office staff to who he was and the likely purpose of his unannounced visit.

When Mr. Flamenco returned from the bank, a warning of Bart's presence was whispered into his ear, negating Bart's advantage of surprise. Nevertheless, Bart confronted Mr. Flamenco about the signs and insisted that the bill be paid. Brushing off the owner's protests that the signs weren't usable, Bart pressed for payment. The conversation grew heated, and Mr. Flamenco not so gently encouraged Bart to remove himself from his office, which Bart reluctantly did. But with his keys imprisoned in the ignition of his car, he could not leave the premises. When Bart's wife ultimately arrived to rescue him, she was the only one within a half a mile who was the least bit amused.

What was really funny was that several times over the pursuing years that same company tried again to order signs from Bart. He shook his head over the audacity of Mr. Flamenco to think that Bart would continue to be a vendor after he had been so unceremoniously booted through the front door. That experience had been indelibly burned into Bart's mind.

The Customer Came Back

Several years after the "key incident", Bart received a routine order from a real estate developer for a banner. As fate would have it, Bart was at the counter when his nemesis, Mr. Flamenco, stepped through the door and asked for the banner. Apparently Mr. Flamenco was a partner with the developer, and Bart had almost done what he swore would never happen. He had almost done business with Mr. Flamenco.

When Mr. Flamenco approached the counter, Bart asked, "Do you remember me?" With a puzzled look Mr. Flamenco responded, "No? Should I?"

"You certainly should! You threw me out of your office one time!"

Mr. Flamenco disavowed all knowledge of the

incident, leaving Bart to wonder just how many other people had been summarily dismissed in the same way. Did this man eject so many people from his premises that any individual incident seemed insignificant?

After reminding Mr. Flamenco of their previous encounter, Bart invited Mr. Flamenco to go back to his partner and explain why it would be necessary to find another sign company to supply their needs. That was one banner that was never going to fly over Baton Rouge!

Gus almost felt sorry for Mr. Flamenco. His ill-advised decision to stiff Bart led to an enhancement of his reputation as a shady character and put him in the uncomfortable situation of having to explain to his partner why he had been blackballed from the premier sign company in the tri-parish area. As Gus's mother often says, "Chickens come home to roost".

Con Artist Customers

While Bart's customers' behaviors did not exactly get them top billing on the Christmas card list, Down South Motors' customer brought the definition of "bad customer" to a whole level. On a beautiful September afternoon, the Saturday after Labor Day, a distinguished looking gentleman strolled into the showroom. Joseph, the dealership's top sales consultant, knew he "wasn't from around here" when the man said he was just looking "aboot" (about). After carefully perusing all of the luxury automobiles in the show room, the gentleman approached the salesman, introduced himself as Mr. Rocancourt, and indicated he had made his selection.

"Are you ready to take her for a spin?" Joseph offered as he shook Mr. Rocancourt's well-manicured hand.

"No thank you. I've done my research, and this is the one I want."

Joseph could hardly believe his good fortune. It was only the middle of the month, and this sale would push him just above his monthly goal. Mr. Rocancourt didn't even haggle on the price. He wanted the car today and would wait in a nearby coffee shop while it was being prepared for delivery. Fortune was clearly smiling on Joseph today. Little did he know that Fortune would not be so kind in just a few days.

Joseph happily introduced Mr. Rocancourt to Mark, the F & I Manager, to finish up the paperwork. Joseph was ecstatic to hear that it wouldn't even be necessary to wait for an answer from one of their lenders. Mr. Rocancourt was prepared to write a check in the amount of $35,612.46. Mark nervously explained to Mr. Rocancourt that the dealership had a policy of calling the bank to verify the funds on all checks over $10,000. Mr. Rocancourt calmly agreed and assured Mark that the funds were there. Mark called the Canadian bank and received assurances that all was in order and the funds were indeed on deposit and available. Forty-five minutes later, Joseph happily watched Mr. Rocancourt drive off the lot with his brand new Sapphire blue convertible.

A Bad Deal

The next Saturday, Joseph was a little surprised to see Mr. Rocancourt drive back into the dealership just after opening time. Joseph extracted himself from a klatch of colleagues and rushed over to open the door for Mr. Rocancourt to exit the vehicle. He was a little taken aback at Mr. Rocancourt's appearance. While he was still well dressed and well groomed, his face looked sallow as if he had not seen the sun in several days.

"How are you Mr. Rocancourt?" Joseph asked.

"Good morning, Joseph. Thank you for asking, but in truth, I'm not well at all. I won't take up your precious time with all of the details, but after I left you last week, I received some very distressing news about my daughter. Suffice it to say that she needs my help, and I am going to have to be with her. She lives in Newfoundland, and I don't know how long my presence will be required. I am flying out this afternoon, and I've come this morning to implore you to allow me to return the car."

"Is there something wrong with the car that we can fix for you?"

"No. As I explained I have a critical family matter to attend to. I can't take the car with me and I might be gone for several months. I simply don't need the car now, and I would like to return it."

"Wow! I've never had a request like this before. Let me bring this to the Sales Manager."

Joseph walked toward the Sales Manager's office with a little less pep in his step. He knew the Sales Manager would do everything he could to accommodate Mr. Rocancourt, and that meant Joseph's commission was in grave danger.

True to Joseph's expectations, the sales manager and Mr. Rocancourt hammered out a deal. The dealership bought the car back for an amount just under $7,000 less than what they had sold it for. After confirming with their bank that his original check had cleared, the dealership wrote Mr. Rocancourt a check for $28,000. He solemnly thanked them, loaded his bags in a taxi and headed for the airport, after stopping at the local bank to cash the dealership's check.

Monday Morning Blues

The next Monday, the sad truth came to light. While the funds did show up in the dealership's account, the bank customer service clerk had failed to notice that the funds were "pending", not "available". The Canadian bank did not honor the fraudulently written check. Mr. Rocancourt was nowhere to be found. The dealership had fallen for one of the basic scams in the con artists playbook.

It was little comfort to them when they discovered that 25 other dealerships in a radius of 500 miles had fallen for the same scheme. The full extent of the dealership's loss was brought to light when they found that, due to exclusion in their policy, this transaction was not covered. The full loss was borne by the dealership and its top salesman, Joseph.

Some more wise words from Gus' mother are appropriate here: "If the deal is too good to be true, it probably isn't." If the customer is too easy, doesn't have any objections and comes to you without references, don't let the dollar signs blind you to the red flags.

Choose your Customers Carefully!: Action Steps

1. Review your customer list and identify the bottom 10% in revenue. Decide which of these customers to fire. An alternative to firing the customers could be to increase your rates for them. If they pay the increased rate, they might leave the bottom 10% list. If they self deselect then you haven't lost a profitable customer. Be careful. Be like a surgeon, not a butcher.

2. Ask your employees which of your customers are the hardest to deal with. Look for signs that the customer disrespects your staff, is extra demanding or is particularly hard to please. Consider firing that customer. Excellent staff members are sometimes hard to find. Demonstrate to them that you "have their back".

IN CLOSING

"Your work is going to fill a large part of your life, and the only way to be truly satisfied is to do what you believe is great work. And the only way to do great work is to love what you do."
-Steve Jobs

Gus finished her five miles on the treadmill and headed to the showers. A half hour later, she hummed an old Johnny Horton tune to herself as she gathered her belongings and headed to her car. Again, the thought of retiring flashed through her mind. Then she smiled. "No Way," she muttered to herself. "This coaching gig is just too much fun!"

ABOUT THE AUTHOR

Karen Johnson is a Certified Public Accountant and Business Coach in Shreveport Louisiana. She lives in nearby Benton with her husband of eighteen years and two sons. She spends her off time attending football games where her sons play in the high school band. Every chance she gets, she spends as much time as possible under the water scuba diving.

Made in the USA
Middletown, DE
29 April 2016